Heirloom BABY KNITS

by Deborah Newton

LEISURE ARTS, INC.
Little Rock, Arkansas

EDITORIAL STAFF
Vice President and Editor-in-Chief:
    Susan White Sullivan
Knit and Crochet Publications Director:
    Lindsay White Glenn
Special Projects Director: Susan Frantz Wiles
Senior Prepress Director: Mark Hawkins
Art Publications Director: Rhonda Shelby
Technical Writer: Linda Daley
Technical Editor: Cathy Hardy
Editorial Writer: Susan McManus Johnson
Art Category Manager: Lora Puls
Graphic Artists: Katherine Laughlin, Becca Snider,
    and Dana Vaughn
Imaging Technician: Stephanie Johnson
Prepress Technician: Janie Marie Wright
Photography Manager: Katherine Laughlin
Contributing Photographers: Jason Masters
    and Ken West
Contributing Photo Stylists: Angela Alexander
    and Sondra Daniel
Publishing Systems Administrator: Becky Riddle
Mac Information Technology Specialist:
    Robert Young

BUSINESS STAFF
President and Chief Executive Officer:
    Rick Barton
Vice President of Sales: Mike Behar
Director of Finance and Administration:
    Laticia Mull Dittrich
Director of Corporate Planning: Anne Martin
National Sales Director: Martha Adams
Creative Services: Chaska Lucas
Information Technology Director: Hermine Linz
Controller: Francis Caple
Vice President, Operations: Jim Dittrich
Retail Customer Service Manager: Stan Raynor
Print Production Manager: Fred F. Pruss

Library of Congress Control Number: 2012932574

ISBN-13: 978-1-60900-190-2

Heirloom BABY

⋀⋁⋀⋁⋀⋁⋀⋁⋀⋁⋀⋁⋀⋁⋀⋁⋀⋁⋀⋁⋀⋁⋀⋁⋀⋁⋀⋁⋀⋁

BABIES ARE SPECIAL LITTLE PEOPLE who inspire our love! Which is why all knitters, myself included, adore making something extra special for babies. So why should a baby sweater, knitted with the anticipation of a little one's happiness, be tossed away when outgrown? I wanted the projects in Heirloom Baby Knits—sweater sets, blankets, and accessories— to have staying power!

As I designed each piece, I envisioned the mothers saving these little knits for other babies as their own babies outgrew them. Imagine—friends and sisters and brothers and cousins all linked together over the years by wearing and sharing a special sweater set or a warm, wooly blanket.

Because baby sweaters are tiny, even those worked in fine yarns knit up quickly. And we knitters are often willing to spend a little more on a deluxe yarn to make a quality baby garment. Yet most moms are surprised to receive luxury knits for their babies. I always include a little card with care instructions— mothers are grateful for this! You'll find these instructions on page 128.

With regards to sizing, it is always desirable to make a garment a size or two larger than the baby at first requires. All babies look charming in oversized garments, and equally sweet when they grow to the point that their garments are a little tight! If a sweater has been well made with beautiful materials, by the time it no longer fits, it is ready to be passed along to another lucky baby.

KNITS
by Deborah Newton

Some of these projects are quick, some demanding—but all are worth the effort! Some will inspire picture-taking for many years to come. Some projects are meant to be whimsical, others more classic. All can be worked in yarns other than those suggested. Note that in the introductions to the projects, I give suggestions for alternate yarns or design variations.

It is my hope that you will find something here for each baby who comes into your life. You may be knitting for your own child, a best friend's baby, or your first grandchild. Or you may be making a sweater for a needy child whom you are unlikely to ever meet. In any case, I hope that over the years ahead, this book will provide you with a range of heirloom projects that will be a delight to knit, to give, and to receive.

Love is always passed on to others in our projects. It is my wish that these carefully planned designs will give you the chance to love and be loved for a very long time, with many, many babies being rewarded by your efforts.

Deborah Newton
Providence, RI
Spring, 2012

DEBORAH NEWTON

MAKING DETAILS COUNT

"When I work on a design collection," says designer Deborah Newton, "I think about how all the projects will appear individually and as part of a group. Both matter, because the knitter is thinking in terms of the wearer's wardrobe. In this case, the wearers are babies, so this collection is extra-special to me. Designing for babies made the work that much more fun."

Deborah creates fabric samples to find the right yarn for each garment. She then relies on experienced knitters to follow her patterns and create the individual garment sections. Deborah carefully assembles and finishes the garments, choosing important details such as buttons. "I achieve so much because of my knitters," says Deborah. "They free me to focus on drafting new ideas."

Recently, Leisure Arts released *Deborah Newton's Warm Weather Knits*, a stunning array of women's sweaters and accessories in the fibers best suited for spring and summer. The book is filled with the exciting new design interpretations that knitters have come to expect in Deborah's creations.

To find #5098 *Deborah Newton's Warm Weather Knits* and more of Deborah's fresh knitting ideas, visit LeisureArts.com.

Deborah would like to extend her special thanks to the expert knitters who worked to make these little heirlooms come to life: Frances Scullin, Patricia Yankee, Lynn Marlow, Lucinda Heller, and Mireille Holland. And thanks also to Barbara Khouri for all her technical expertise.

TABLE OF CONTENTS

BUTTON-BLUE

Side-Button Vest and Socks

This precious little vest is knitted all in one piece, with side and shoulder button details. It is a useful sweater that mothers will reach for again and again. Your favorite baby will have room to grow since the sweater's rib-like pattern expands. My favorite ribbed socks add something extra to the set. Whenever you are making an heirloom sweater, search for the best buttons you can find. Today it is easy to choose new or vintage buttons at online sites that sell supplies, such as etsy.com. I am addicted to buttons, and I have a huge stash of all kinds in small sizes for baby duds. I love oversized buttons too—they add a wee bit of clownish whimsy that makes a little guy or girl even cuter!

SIZES
To fit sizes 6{12-18-24} months
Sample worked in size 12 months.

FINISHED MEASUREMENTS
Chest at underarm:
23{24-25¹/₂-27¹/₂}"/
58.5{61-65-70} cm
Length:
11{12-13-14}"/
28{30.5-33-35.5} cm

Size Note: Instructions for Vest
are written for size 6 months with
sizes 12, 18 and 24 months in
braces { }. Instructions will be easier
to read if you circle all the numbers
pertaining to your baby's size.
If only one number is given, it
applies to all sizes.

MATERIALS
ROWAN "Cashsoft DK"
(57% Extra Merino Wool, 33%
Acrylic Microfiber, 10% Cashmere;
50 grams/126 yards)
   Color #805 (Cloud):
      4{4-4-5} balls
Straight knitting needles,
   size 6 (4 mm) **or** size needed
   to obtain gauge
24" (61 cm) Circular knitting
   needle, size 6 (4 mm)
Double-pointed knitting needles
   (set of 5), size 6 (4 mm)
   (for socks)
Stitch holder
Tapestry needle
³/₄" (19 mm) Buttons - 8

GAUGE
Over Ribbed Leaf pattern
with size 6 needles:
28 sts and 30 rows = 4" (10 cm)
Take time to save time, check
your gauge.

Techniques used:
• tbl *(Fig. 3, page 115)*
• YO *(Fig. 5a, page 117)*
• K2 tog *(Fig. 8, page 119)*
• SSK *(Figs. 10a-c, page 120)*

PATTERN STITCHES
STOCKINETTE STITCH (St st):
Any number of sts
Knit RS rows, purl WS rows.

RIBBED LEAF PATTERN: Multiple of 10 sts plus 1
Right Twist (RT): K2 tog, leave sts
on needle, then insert RH needle
between 2 sts just knitted tog and
knit the first st again, then slip both
sts from LH needle.
Left Twist (LT): Knit into the back
of the second st, then knit the first
st, and slip both sts off needle tog.

Rows 1, 3, 5, 7 and 9 (WS): P1,
* K2, P5, K2, P1; rep from * across.
Rows 2, 4, 6, 8 and 10: K1 tbl, * P2,
RT, K1, LT, P2, K1 tbl; rep from *
across.
Rows 11, 13, 15, 17 and 19 (WS):
P3, * K2, P1, K2, P5; rep from
* across, end last rep P3.
Rows 12, 14, 16, 18 and 20: K1,
* LT, P2, K1 tbl, P2, RT, K1; rep from
* across.
Rep Rows 1-20 for Ribbed Leaf
pattern.

VEST
BODY

Note: Body is worked in one piece to armholes, then front and back are worked separately.

With circular needle, cast on 163{173-183-193} sts.

Work back and forth.

Establish Patterns (WS): P1 (St st edge st), work Row 1 of Ribbed Leaf pattern over 161{171-181-191} sts, end P1 (St st edge st).

Work even until piece measures 5$\frac{1}{2}${6-6$\frac{1}{2}$-7}"/14{15-16.5-18} cm, end with a RS row.

Divide for Armholes (WS): Mark center st.
Work to center marked st, slip these 81{86-91-96} sts just worked onto a st holder for Back, then join a second ball of yarn and bind off center st, work as established to end.

Front: Now work front and back separately.

Next Row (RS): Keeping in pattern, bind off 3 sts at the beginning of the row, work to end — 78{83-88-93} sts.

Next Row (WS): Bind off 3{2-3-2} sts, work to end — 75{81-85-91} sts.

Bind off 0{0-3-0} sts at the beginning of the next 2 rows *(see Zeros, page 114)*, then 2 sts at the beginning of the next 4{4-2-6} rows — 67{73-75-79} sts.

Keeping first and last st of every row in St st, work in pattern as established over center 65{71-73-77} sts until armhole measures 2$\frac{1}{2}${3-3$\frac{1}{2}$-4}"/6.5{7.5-9-10} cm, end with a WS row.

Neck Shaping: Mark center 19 sts. Work to center 19 sts, join a second ball of yarn and bind off center sts, work as established to end — 24{27-28-30} sts remain each side.

Working both sides at the same time with separate balls of yarn, bind off 2 sts from each Neck edge, 5 times — 14{17-18-20} sts remain each side.

Work even until armholes measure 5$\frac{1}{2}${6-6$\frac{1}{2}$-7}"/14{15-16.5-18} cm, end with a WS row.

Bind off remaining 14{17-18-20} sts each side for shoulders.

Back: With RS facing, slip 81{86-91-96} sts from Back st holder onto straight needles.
Attach yarn at beginning of RS row at armhole edge.

Next Row (RS): Keeping in pattern, bind off 3 sts at the beginning of the row, work to end — 78{83-88-93} sts.

Next Row (WS): Bind off 3{2-3-2} sts, work to end — 75{81-85-91} sts.

Bind off 0{0-3-0} sts at the beginning of the next 2 rows, then 2 sts at the beginning of the next 4{4-2-6} rows — 67{73-75-79} sts.

Keeping first and last st of every row in St st, work in pattern as established over center 65{71-73-77} sts until armhole measures 4$\frac{1}{2}${5-5$\frac{1}{2}$-6}"/11.5{12.5-14-15} cm, end with a WS row.

Neck Shaping: Mark center 19 sts. Work to center 19 sts, join a second ball of yarn and bind off center sts, work to end — 24{27-28-30} sts remain each side.

Working both sides at the same time with separate balls of yarn, bind off 5 sts from each Neck edge, 2 times — 14{17-18-20} sts remain each side.

Work even until armholes measure 5$\frac{1}{2}${6-6$\frac{1}{2}$-7}"/14{15-16.5-18} cm, end with a WS row.

Bind off remaining 14{17-18-20} sts each side for shoulders.

FINISHING

Right Armhole Trim: With RS facing, using straight needles and starting at shoulder, pick up 60{64-68-72} sts evenly spaced around entire armhole edge *(Figs. 14a & b, page 123)*.

Knit 2 rows.

Bind off all sts in knit.

Sew Front to Back at right shoulder.

Left Back Armhole Trim: With RS facing, using straight needles and starting at shoulder, pick up 31{33-35-37} sts evenly spaced along armhole edge.

Knit 2 rows.

Bind off all sts in knit.

Left Front Armhole Trim: With RS facing, using straight needles and starting at underarm, pick up 31{33-35-37} sts evenly spaced along armhole edge.

Knit 2 rows.

Bind off all sts in knit.

Neckline Trim: With RS facing, using straight needles and starting at open shoulder, pick up 52 sts evenly spaced along Front Neck, then 36 sts evenly spaced along Back Neck — 88 sts.

Knit 2 rows.

Bind off all sts in knit.

Back Left Shoulder Button Band: With RS facing and straight needles, pick up 16{18-18-20} sts evenly spaced along back left shoulder.

Knit 2 rows.

Bind off all sts in knit.

Front Left Buttonhole Band: With RS facing and straight needles, pick up 16{18-18-20} sts evenly spaced along front left shoulder.

Next (buttonhole) Row (WS): K 0{1-1-2}, K2 tog, YO, SSK, (K2, K2 tog, YO, SSK) twice, K 0{1-1-2} — 13{15-15-17} sts.

Next Row (RS): Knit each st and (K1, P1) into each YO of the previous row — 16{18-18-20} sts.

Knit 2 rows.

Bind off all sts in knit.

Left Back Side Button Band: With RS facing and straight needles, pick up 31{35-39-43} sts evenly spaced along left back side edge.

Knit 2 rows.

Bind off all sts in knit.

Left Front Side Buttonhole Band: With RS facing and straight needles, pick up 31{35-39-43} sts evenly spaced along left front side edge.

Next (buttonhole) Row (WS): K1{3-4-4}, K2 tog, YO, SSK, [K4{4-5-6}, K2 tog, YO, SSK] 3 times, K2{4-4-5} — 27{31-35-39} sts.

Next Row (RS): Knit each st and (K1, P1) into each YO of the previous row — 31{35-39-43} sts.

Knit 2 rows.

Bind off all sts in knit.

Sew buttons opposite buttonholes on shoulder and sides.

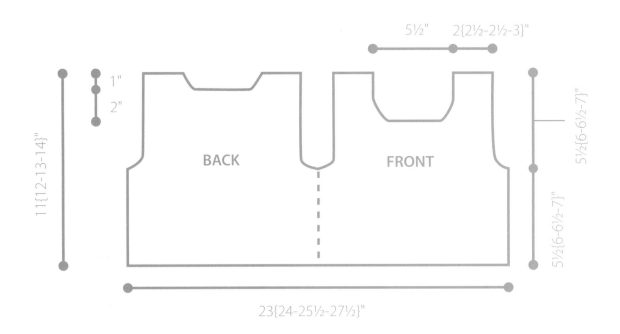

SOCKS
To fit size 12 months

PATTERN STITCH: Multiple of 4 sts
Rnds 1-4: * K2, P2; rep from * around.
Rnds 5-8: * K1, P2, K1; rep from * around.
Rnds 9-12: * P2, K2; rep from * around.
Rnds 13-16: * P1, K2, P1; rep from * around.
Rep Rnds 1-16 for pattern.

LEG
With dpns, cast on 36 sts and divide sts evenly onto 4 dpns (9 sts on each needle) *(Fig. 2, page 115)*.

Rep Rnds 1-16 of Pattern st until piece measures 6" (15 cm).

TOE
Rnd 1: Knit around.

Rnd 2: * K1, SSK, K6; rep from * around — 32 sts.

Rnd 3: Knit around.

Rnd 4: * K2, SSK, K4; rep from * around — 28 sts.

Rnd 5: Knit around.

Rnd 6: * K3, SSK, K2; rep from * around — 24 sts.

Rnd 7: * K4, SSK; rep from * around — 20 sts.

Divide sts evenly on 2 needles and graft together *(Figs. 17a & b, page 125)*.

CARAMEL CONFECTION
Patterned Pullover with Mitered Corners

I come from a Swedish background, and I adore all the colorwork patterns of Scandinavian patterning. The bold repeating motif in this sweater has an almost floral feel to it—like a "Marimekko®"-brand textile-print poppy in simplified form—but is suited to a boy or girl. I find a simple tabard sweater like this so rewarding to knit. First there is the pleasure of the stranded colorwork rectangle; then that is followed by the trim around the edges. Mitered corners make this special. A luxury yarn with a halo to it gives this sweater a soft look, and a crisp wool would create stronger contrast and work just as well. To alter this pattern and make it your own, why not work the motifs in several colors? Or stripe the edgings? Or make the tabard longer and more coat-like?

SIZES
To fit sizes 6{12-18-24} months
Sample worked in size 12 months.

FINISHED MEASUREMENTS
Chest at underarm:
24{26-28-30}"/
61{66-71-76} cm
Length:
13{13½-14-14½}"/
33{34.5-35.5-37} cm
Sleeve width at upper arm:
11{12-13-14}"/
28{30.5-33-35.5} cm

Size Note: Instructions are written
for size 6 months with sizes 12,
18 and 24 months in braces { }.
Instructions will be easier to
read if you circle all the numbers
pertaining to your baby's size. If
only one number is given, it applies
to all sizes.

MATERIALS
CLASSIC ELITE "Fresco"
(60% Wool, 30% Baby Alpaca,
10% Angora; 50 grams/164 yards)
in colors:
A #5336 (Oatmeal):
2{2-3-3} hanks
B #5350 (Ginger): 2{2-3-3} hanks
Straight knitting needles,
sizes 6 (4 mm), 7 (4.5 mm) **and**
8 (5 mm) **or** sizes needed to
obtain gauges
24" (61 cm) Circular knitting
needle, size 7 (4.5 mm)
Stitch markers
Tapestry needle

GAUGE
Over Color Work Chart
with size 8 needles:
24 sts and 24 rows = 4" (10 cm)
Over Broken Rib pattern
with size 7 needles:
24 sts and 32 rows = 4" (10 cm)
Take time to save time, check your
gauge.

Technique used:
• M1 *(Figs. 7a & b, page 119)*

PATTERN STITCHES
STOCKINETTE STITCH (St st):
Any number of sts
Knit RS rows, purl WS rows.

GARTER STITCH:
Any number of sts
Knit every row.

BROKEN RIB PATTERN: Multiple
of 4 sts plus 2
Row 1 (RS): K2, * P2, K2; rep from
* across.
Row 2: P2, * K2, P2; rep from
* across.
Row 3: Knit across.
Row 4: Purl across.
Rep Rows 1-4 for Broken Rib
pattern.

PULLOVER
COLOR WORK SQUARE
(Make 2)

With size 8 needles and B, cast on 59 sts.

Knit one RS row. Purl one WS row.

Next Row (RS): Follow chart working 14 st rep (4 times).

Work the 14 rows of chart 4 times, and then work Row 1 again.

With B, bind off all sts in purl.

BACK

With RS of Color Work Square facing, using size 7 straight needles and A, pick up 48 sts evenly spaced across bound off edge *(Fig. 14b, page 123)*.

Knit 3 rows.

Neck Shaping (RS): K7, join a second ball of yarn and bind off center 34 sts, knit to end — 7 sts remain each side.

Working both sides at the same time with separate balls of yarn, work in Garter st until piece measures 11^1/$_2$" (29 cm), end with a WS row.

Bind off 7 sts each side for shoulders.

Tabbard Sides: With RS facing, using circular needle and A, and starting at shoulder, pick up 60 sts evenly spaced along side edge *(Fig. 14a, page 123)*, place marker (PM) *(see Markers, page 114)*, pick up one st in corner, PM, pick up 48 sts evenly spaced along bottom edge, PM, pick up one st in corner, PM, pick up 60 sts evenly spaced along side edge to shoulder — 170 sts.

Next Row (WS): Knit 60 sts, slip marker, P1, slip marker, knit 48 sts, slip marker, P1, slip marker, knit 60 sts.

Next (increase) Row (RS): * Knit across to marker (keep in Garter st), M1, slip marker, K1 (corner st, keep in St st), slip marker, M1; repeat from * once more, knit to end — 174 sts.

Working increases into Garter st, work as established and rep increase row every RS row until Tabbard Sides measure 1^1/$_4${1^3/$_4$-2^1/$_4$-2^3/$_4$}"/3{4.5-5.5-7} cm, end with a WS row.

Change to B and work for 2 rows more.

Bind off all sts in knit.

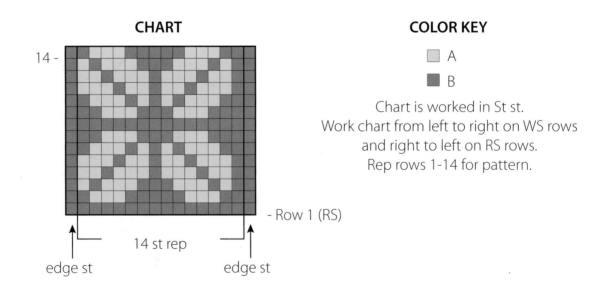

CHART

14 -

- Row 1 (RS)

edge st   14 st rep   edge st

COLOR KEY

☐ A

■ B

Chart is worked in St st.
Work chart from left to right on WS rows
and right to left on RS rows.
Rep rows 1-14 for pattern.

FRONT
Work same as Back.

SLEEVE (Make 2)
With size 7 needles and B,
cast on 38{38-42-46} sts.

Purl WS row.

Next Row (RS): K2 (St st edge sts),
work Row 1 of Broken Rib pattern
over 34{34-38-42} sts, end K2 (St st
edge sts).

Work even for 3 rows.

Next (increase) Row (RS): K2, M1,
work to last 2 sts, M1, end K2 —
40{40-44-48} sts.

Working increases into Broken Rib
pattern, work WS row.

Next (increase) Row (RS): K2, M1,
work to last 2 sts, M1, end K2 —
42{42-46-50} sts.

Work even for 3 rows.

Rep the last 6 rows, 6{7-7-6} times
more; then rep increase row every
RS row 0{1-2-5} time(s) *(see Zeros,
page 114)* — 66{72-78-84} sts.

Work even until Sleeve measures
7¹/₂" (19 cm), end with a WS row.

Bind off all sts.

FINISHING
Sew Front to Back at shoulders.

Neckline Trim: With RS facing, using size 6 needles and B, and starting at neckline corner, pick up 15 sts evenly spaced along side of neckline.

Knit 11 rows.

Bind off all sts in knit.

Sew edge of trim to Front and Back neckline where they meet.

Rep on other side.

Mark $5^1/_2${6-6$^1/_2$-7}"/ 14{15-16.5-18} cm down from shoulder on Front and Back.

Sew Sleeves between markers. Sew Sleeve seams.

Join Front to Back at sides, 2$^1/_2$" (6.5 cm) down from underarm. Leave remainder of side open.

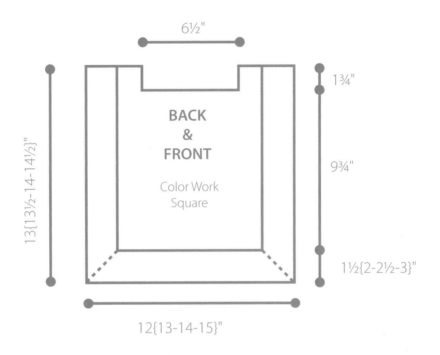

6½"

1¾"

BACK
&
FRONT

Color Work
Square

9¾"

13{13½-14-14½}"

1½{2-2½-3}"

12{13-14-15}"

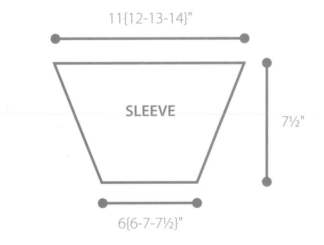

11{12-13-14}"

SLEEVE

7½"

6{6-7-7½}"

COLLEGIATE CONTRAST
Cardigan, Cropped Pants, and Socks

Playful stripes are a natural for babies. Here, my inspiration was a cabled tennis sweater with the stripes confined to the edges. The cables are easy to knit, and the cardigan's boxy shape is simple to assemble. Comfy, easy-fit pants have cables down the sides. The ribbed socks, featured here and in two other patterns, are just tubes of diagonal ribbing. For variation, you could eliminate the stripes. Or to emphasize the striped effect, work the body of the sweater and/or pants in stripes, too! For narrow stripes, work 2 or 4 rows of each color. For broad stripes, work 6 to 8 rows. I also suggest that you could work the cardigan as shown, but make the pants red—with purple stripes! This set is in a smooth bamboo/wool blend that is warm yet silky to the touch.

SIZES
To fit sizes 12{18-24-30} months
Sample worked in size 12 months.

FINISHED MEASUREMENTS
Cardigan:
  Chest at underarm:
    24{26-28-30}"/
    61{66-71-76} cm
  Length:
    12{13-14-15}"/
    30.5{33-35.5-38} cm
  Sleeve width at upper arm:
    11{12½-13½-14½}"/
    28{32-34.5-37} cm
Pants:
  Waist:
    21{24-26-28}"/
    53.5{61-66-71} cm
  Length:
    12{13-14-15}"/
    30.5{33-35.5-38} cm

Size Note: Instructions for Cardigan and Pants are written for size 12 months with sizes 18, 24 and 30 months in braces { }. Instructions will be easier to read if you circle all the numbers pertaining to your baby's size. If only one number is given, it applies to all sizes.

MATERIALS
CLASSIC ELITE
"Wool Bam Boo"
(50% Bamboo Viscose/50% Wool; 50 grams/118 yards) in colors:
  MC #1632 (Italian Plum):
    8{9-10-12} balls
  A #1641 (Havana Red): 1 ball
  B #1648 (Denim Blue): 1 ball
Straight knitting needles,
  size 6 (4 mm) **or** size needed
  to obtain gauge
16" (40.5 cm) Circular knitting
  needle, size 6 (4 mm)
Crochet hook, size G (4 mm)
  (for Pants)
Double-pointed knitting needles
  (set of 5), size 6 (4 mm)
  (for Socks)
Cable needle
Stitch markers (for Pants)
Tapestry needle
⁹⁄₁₆" (14 mm) Buttons - 8

GAUGE
Over Rev St st with size 6 needles:
22 sts and 38 rows = 4" (10 cm)
Take time to save time, check your gauge.

Techniques used:
• YO *(Figs. 5a & c, page 117)*
• M1 *(Figs. 7a & b, page 119)*
• K2 tog *(Fig. 8, page 119)*
• P2 tog *(Fig. 9, page 119)*
• SSK *(Figs. 10a-c, page 120)*

PATTERN STITCHES
STOCKINETTE STITCH (St st):
Any number of sts
Knit RS rows, purl WS rows.

REVERSE STOCKINETTE STITCH
(Rev St st): Any number of sts
Purl RS rows, knit WS rows.

RIGHT CABLE: Over 8 sts
Rows 1 and 3 (RS): K8.
Rows 2 and 4: P8.
Row 5: Slip 4 sts onto cn and hold in back, K4, K4 from cn.
Rows 6 and 8: P8.
Rows 7 and 9: K8.
Row 10: P8.
Rep Rows 1-10 for Right Cable.

LEFT CABLE: Over 8 sts
Rows 1 and 3 (RS): K8.
Rows 2 and 4: P8.
Row 5: Slip 4 sts onto cn and hold in front, K4, K4 from cn.
Rows 6 and 8: P8.
Rows 7 and 9: K8.
Row 10: P8.
Rep Rows 1-10 for Left Cable.

TEXTURED PANEL: Panel of 18 sts

Rows 1, 3, 5, 7 and 9 (RS): P3, (K2, P3) 3 times.

Rows 2, 4, 6 and 8: K3, (P2, K3) 3 times.

Row 10: K3, P 12, K3.

Rows 11 and 13: Purl across.

Row 12: Knit across.

Rows 14 and 16: K3, P 12, K3.

Row 15: P3, K 12, P3.

Rows 17 and 19: Purl across.

Row 18: Knit across.

Rows 20 and 22: K3, P 12, K3.

Row 21: P3, K 12, P3.

Rows 23 and 25: Purl across.

Row 24: Knit across.

Row 26: K3, P 12, K3.

Rep Rows 1-26 for Textured Panel.

CARDIGAN
BACK

With straight needles and MC, cast on 86{90-96-102} sts.

Establish Patterns (RS): K2 (St st edge sts), P3{5-8-11}, work Row 1 of Right Cable over 8 sts, work Row 1 of Textured Panel over 18 sts, work Row 1 of Left Cable over 8 sts, P3, K2, P3, work Row 1 of Right Cable over 8 sts, work Row 1 of Textured Panel over 18 sts, work Row 1 of Left Cable over 8 sts, P3{5-8-11}, end K2 (St st edge sts).

Next Row (WS): P2 (St st edge sts), K3{5-8-11}, work Row 2 of Left Cable over 8 sts, work Row 2 of Textured Panel over 18 sts, work Row 2 of Right Cable over 8 sts, K3, P2, K3, work Row 2 of Left Cable over 8 sts, work Row 2 of Textured Panel over 18 sts, work Row 2 of Right Cable over 8 sts, K3{5-8-11}, end P2 (St st edge sts).

Work even as established until piece measures 11½{12½-13½-14½}"/ 29{32-34.5-37} cm, end with a WS row.

Neck Shaping (RS): Mark center 40 sts.
Work to center 40 sts, join a second ball of yarn and bind off center sts, work as established to end — 23{25-28-31} sts remain each side.

Working both sides at the same time with separate balls of yarn, work even for 3 rows more, piece measures approximately 12{13-14-15}"/30.5{33-35.5-38} cm.

Bind off remaining 23{25-28-31} sts from each shoulder.

LEFT FRONT

With straight needles and MC, cast on 44{46-49-52} sts.

Establish Patterns (RS): K2 (St st edge sts), P3{5-8-11}, work Row 1 of Right Cable over 8 sts, work Row 1 of Textured Panel over 18 sts, work Row 1 of Left Cable over 8 sts, P3, end K2 (St st edge sts).

Next Row (WS): P2 (St st edge sts), K3, work Row 2 of Left Cable over 8 sts, work Row 2 of Textured Panel over 18 sts, work Row 2 of Right Cable over 8 sts, K3{5-8-11} sts, end P2 (St st edge sts).

Work even as establish until piece measures 10{11-12-13}"/ 25.5{28-30.5-33} cm, end with a RS row.

Neck Shaping (WS): Bind off 13 sts at the beginning of the next WS row, then 2 sts at the beginning of the next 4 WS rows — 23{25-28-31} sts.

Work even until Left Front measures same as Back to shoulder.

Bind off remaining 23{25-28-31} sts for shoulder on next RS row.

RIGHT FRONT

Work same as for Left Front, reversing patterns and Neck Shaping, and beginning Neck Shaping one row sooner, on a RS row.

SLEEVE (Make 2)

With straight needles and MC, cast on 44{50-50-56} sts.

Establish Patterns (RS): K2 (St st edge sts), P3{6-6-9}, work Row 1 of Right Cable over 8 sts, work Row 1 of Textured Panel over 18 sts, work Row 1 of Left Cable over 8 sts, P3{6-6-9}, end K2 (St st edge sts).

Next Row (WS): P2 (St st edge sts), K3{6-6-9}, work Row 2 of Left Cable over 8 sts, work Row 2 of Textured Panel over 18 sts, work Row 2 of Right Cable over 8 sts, K3{6-6-9}, end P2 (St st edge sts).

Work even as established for 4 rows more.

Next (increase) Row (RS): K2, M1, work as established to last 2 sts, M1, end K2 — 46{52-52-58} sts.

Working increases into Rev St st, rep increase row every 4th row 11{12-14-14} times more — 68{76-80-86} sts.

Work even in patterns as established until Sleeve measures 8{9-10-11}"/20.5{23-25.5-28} cm, end with a WS row.

Bind off all sts in pattern.

Trim: With RS facing, using straight needles and B, pick up 28{32-32-36} sts evenly spaced across cast on edge *(Figs. 14a & b, page 123)*.

K2 rows.

Change to A and knit 1 row.

Bind off all sts in knit.

FINISHING

Sew Fronts to Back at shoulders.

Mark 5¾{6¼-6¾-7¼}"/ 14.5{16-17-18.5} cm down from shoulder on Front and Back.

Sew Sleeves between markers. Sew Sleeve and side seams.

Neckline Trim: With RS facing, using straight needles and B, pick up 94 sts evenly spaced around neckline.

Next Row (WS): P2, * K2, P2; rep from * across.

Work in rib as established for 2 rows more.

Change to A and work in rib for 1 row more.

Bind off all sts in rib.

Lower Body Edge: With RS facing, using circular needle and B, pick up 210{222-234-246} sts evenly spaced around lower edge.

Next Row (WS): P2, * K2, P2; rep from * across.

Work in rib as established for 2 rows more.

Change to A and work in rib for 1 row more.

Bind off all sts in rib.

Left Front Button Band (for boy, work on Right Front): With RS facing, using straight needles and B, pick up 56{60-64-68} sts evenly spaced along edge.

Knit 3 rows.

Change to A and knit 1 row.

Bind off all sts in knit.

Right Front Buttonhole Band (for boy, work on Left Front): With RS facing, using straight needles and B, pick up 56{60-64-68} sts evenly spaced along edge.

Buttonhole Row (WS): K2{3-2-4}, K2 tog, YO, SSK, * K3{3-4-4}, K2 tog, YO, SSK; repeat from * across, end K1{4-2-4} — 48{52-56-60} sts.

Next Row (RS): Knit each st and (K1, P1) into each YO of the previous row — 56{60-64-68} sts.

Knit 1 row.

Change to A and knit 1 row.

Bind off all sts in knit.

Sew buttons opposite buttonholes.

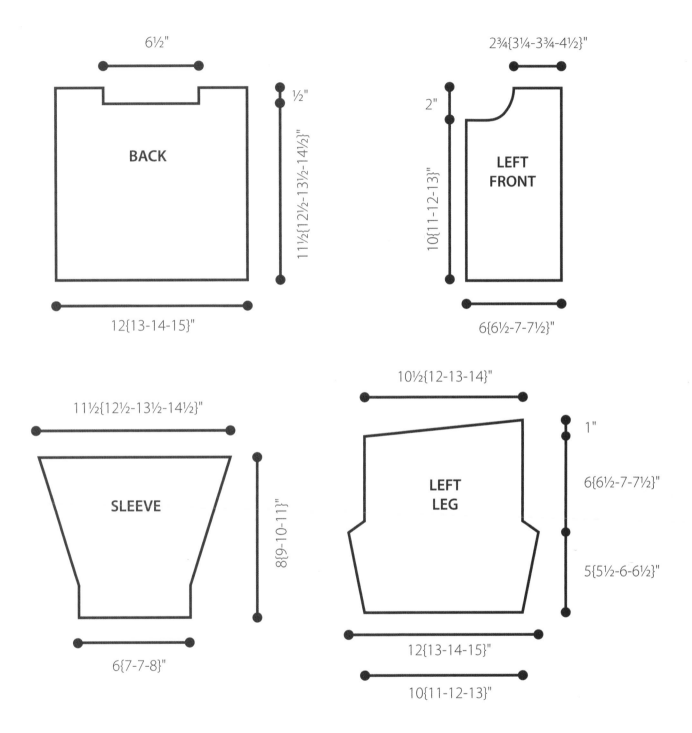

BACK

6½"

½"

11½{12½-13½-14½}"

12{13-14-15}"

LEFT FRONT

2¾{3¼-3¾-4½}"

2"

10{11-12-13}"

6{6½-7-7½}"

SLEEVE

11½{12½-13½-14½}"

8{9-10-11}"

6{7-7-8}"

LEFT LEG

10½{12-13-14}"

1"

6{6½-7-7½}"

5{5½-6-6½}"

12{13-14-15}"

10{11-12-13}"

CROPPED PANTS
LEFT LEG

With straight needles and MC, cast on 68{74-80-86} sts.

Establish Patterns (RS): K2 (St st edge sts), P 15{18-21-24}, work Row 1 of Right Cable over 8 sts, work Row 1 of Textured Panel over 18 sts, work Row 1 of Left Cable over 8 sts, P 15{18-21-24}, end K2 (St st edge sts).

Next Row (WS): P2 (St st edge sts), K 15{18-21-24}, work Row 2 of Left Cable over 8 sts, work Row 2 of Textured Panel over 18 sts, work Row 2 of Right Cable over 8 sts, K 15{18-21-24}, end P2 (St st edge sts).

Work even in established patterns for 4 rows more.

Next (increase) Row (RS): K2, M1, work as established to last 2 sts, M1, K2 — 70{76-82-88} sts.

Working increases into Rev St st, rep increase row every 4th row 4 times more — 78{84-90-96} sts.

Work even until piece measures 5{5½-6-6½}"/12.5{14-15-16.5} cm, end with a WS row.

Note: Tie a yarn marker at the center of this next crotch row.

Shape Crotch (RS): Bind off 2 sts at the beginning of the next 6 rows — 66{72-78-84} sts.

Next Row (RS): K2 (St st edge sts), work in patterns to last 2 sts, K2 (St st edge sts).

Work as established until piece measures 6{6½-7-7½}"/15{16.5-18-19} cm from marker, end with a RS row.

Waist Shaping: Bind off 14{15-16-17} sts, work to end — 52{57-62-67} sts.

Continue in patterns and bind off 13{15-16-17} sts at the beginning of the next 4{1-2-3} WS row(s), then 0{14-15-16} sts at the beginning of the next 0{3-2-1} WS row(s) *(see Zeros, page 114)*.

TRIM

With RS facing, using straight needles and B, pick up 66{70-74-78} sts evenly spaced across cast on edge.

Next Row (WS): P2, * K2, P2; rep from * across.

Work in rib as established for 2 rows more.

Change to A and work in rib for 1 row more.

Bind off all sts in rib.

RIGHT LEG

Work same as for Left Leg, beginning Waist Shaping one row sooner, on a RS row.

FINISHING

Sew pant and crotch seams.

Waistline Rib: With RS facing, using circular needle and B, pick up 128{144-160-168} sts evenly spaced around waistline of pants. Join and place marker for beginning of rnd *(see Markers, page 114)*.

Next Rnd: * K2, P2; rep from * around.

Work in established rib for 3 rnds more.

Next (eyelet) Rnd: * K2, YO, P2 tog, K2, P2; rep from * around.

Work in established rib for 4 rnds more.

Change to A and work 1 rnd more.

Bind off all sts in rib.

Cord: With crochet hook, make a chain 36{38-40-42}"/91.5{96.5-101.5-106.5} cm long *(Fig. 19, page 127)*.

Slip st in second chain from hook *(Fig. 20, page 127)* and in each chain across.

Cut yarn and fasten off.

Beginning at center front, thread cord through eyelet rnd of Pants.

SOCKS

To fit size 12 months

PATTERN STITCH: Multiple of 4 sts

Rnds 1-4: * K2, P2; rep from * around.

Rnds 5-8: * K1, P2, K1; rep from * around.

Rnds 9-12: * P2, K2; rep from * around.

Rnds 13-16: * P1, K2, P1; rep from * around.

Rep Rnds 1-16 for pattern.

LEG

With dpns and B, cast on 36 sts and divide sts evenly onto 4 dpns (9 sts on each needle) *(Fig. 2, page 115)*.

Work Rnds 1-4 of Pattern st.

Change to A and continue through Rnd 16, then rep Rnds 1-16 until piece measures 6" (15 cm).

TOE

Rnd 1: Change to B and knit around.

Rnd 2: * K1, SSK, K6; rep from * around — 32 sts.

Rnd 3: Knit around.

Rnd 4: * K2, SSK, K4; rep from * around — 28 sts.

Rnd 5: Knit around.

Rnd 6: * K3, SSK, K2; rep from * around — 24 sts.

Rnd 7: * K4, SSK; rep from * around — 20 sts.

Divide sts evenly on 2 needles and graft together *(Figs. 17a & b, page 125)*.

FIELD OF FLOWERS
Ruffled Vest and Blanket

This pattern stitch, designed by the remarkable Barbara Walker for her treasury called *Charted Knitting Patterns* (Schoolhouse Press) is one of my favorites. The pattern drops diamond-dots of flowers (that is how I see them!) onto easy garter stitch fabric. For the blanket, I alternated large blocks of the pattern, knitting them in different directions and picking up squares along edges of others. If you use only a single color, your set will still have plenty of detail in the texture. I used one of the large blocks for the body of the vest—for ease of knitting, larger sizes just have extra garter stitches at the sides. This very feminine set is knit in a machine-washable acrylic/rayon blend that has a drapey, silky effect well-suited for spring or summer. For a winter-weight set with the top worn over a turtleneck, try a wool or wool blend.

SIZES
To fit sizes 6{12-18-24} months
Sample worked in size 12 months.

FINISHED MEASUREMENTS
Vest:
   Chest at underarm:
      20{22-24-26}"/
      51{56-61-66} cm
   Length:
      9{9¹/₂-10¹/₂-11¹/₂}"/
      23{24-26.5-29} cm
Blanket (after finishing):
   33" wide x 42" long
   (84 cm x 106.5 cm)

Size Note: Instructions for Vest are written for size 6 months with sizes 12, 18 and 24 months in braces { }. Instructions will be easier to read if you circle all the numbers pertaining to your baby's size. If only one number is given, it applies to all sizes.

MATERIALS
CARON INTERNATIONAL "Spa"
(75% Microdenier Acrylic, 25% Rayon from Bamboo; 85 grams/251 yards) in colors:
   Vest:
      #0004 (Green Sheen):
         1{1-2-2} skein(s)
   Blanket:
      A #0005 (Ocean Spray):
         1 skein
      B #0002 (Coral Lipstick):
         1 skein
      C #0001 (Rose Bisque): 1 skein
      D #0004 (Green Sheen):
         1 skein
Straight knitting needles, size 7 (4.5 mm) **or** size needed to obtain gauge
24" (61 cm) Circular knitting needle, size 7 (4.5 mm)
Stitch markers
Tapestry needle

GAUGE
Over Garter and Lace pattern with size 7 needles:
21 sts and 32 rows = 4" (10 cm)
Take time to save time, check your gauge.

Techniques used:
• YO (*Fig. 5a, page 117*)
• K2 tog (*Fig. 8, page 119*)
• SSK (*Figs. 10a-c, page 120*)
• Slip 1 as if to **knit**, K2 tog, PSSO (*Figs. 12a & b, page 121*)

PATTERN STITCHES
GARTER STITCH: Any number of sts
Knit every row.

LACE RIB: Multiple of 7 sts plus 8
Rows 1 and 3 (WS): P2, K4, * P3, K4; rep from * across, end P2.
Row 2 (RS): K2, P4, * K1, YO, SSK, P4; rep from * across, end K2.
Row 4 (RS): K2, P4, * K2 tog, YO, K1, P4; rep from * across, end K2.
Rep Rows 1-4 for Lace Rib.

GARTER AND LACE PATTERN: Multiple of 16 sts plus 15
Row 1 (RS): K5, * K2 tog, YO, K1, YO, SSK, K 11; rep from * across, end last rep K5.
Row 2 (WS): K5, P5, K5, * P1, K5, P5, K5; rep from * across.
Row 3: K4, * K2 tog, YO, K3, YO, SSK, K9; rep from * across, end last rep K4.
Row 4: K4, P7, K4, * P1, K4, P7, K4; rep from * across.
Row 5: K3, K2 tog, YO, K5, YO, SSK, * K7, K2 tog, YO, K5, YO, SSK; rep from * across, end K3.
Row 6: K3, P9, K3, * P1, K3, P9, K3; rep from * across.
Row 7: K4, * YO, SSK, K3, K2 tog, YO, K9; rep from * across, end last rep K4.

Row 8: K4, P7, K4, * P1, K4, P7, K4; rep from * across.

Row 9: K5, * K2 tog, YO, K1, YO, SSK, K 11; rep from * across, end last rep K5.

Row 10: K5, P5, K5, * P1, K5, P5, K5; rep from * across.

Row 11: K6, * YO, slip 1, K2 tog, PSSO, YO, K 13; rep from * across, end last rep K6.

Row 12: K6, P3, * (K5, P3) twice; rep from * across, end K6.

Row 13: K 13, * K2 tog, YO, K1, YO, SSK, K 11; rep from * across, end last rep K 13.

Row 14: K7, P1, * K5, P5, K5, P1; rep from * across, end K7.

Row 15: K 12, * K2 tog, YO, K3, YO, SSK, K9; rep from * across, end K3.

Row 16: K7, P1, * K4, P7, K4, P1; rep from * across, end K7.

Row 17: K 11, * K2 tog, YO, K5, YO, SSK, K7; rep from * across, end last rep K 11.

Row 18: K7, P1, * K3, P9, K3, P1; rep from * across, end K7.

Row 19: K 12, * YO, SSK, K3, K2 tog, YO, K9; rep from * across, end last rep K 12.

Row 20: K7, P1, * K4, P7, K4, P1; rep from * across, end K7.

Row 21: K 13, * YO, SSK, K1, K2 tog, YO, K 11; rep from * across, end last rep K 13.

Row 22: K7, P1, * K5, P5, K5, P1; rep from * across, end K7.

Row 23: K 14, * YO, slip 1, K2 tog, PSSO, YO, K 13; rep from * across, end last rep K 14.

Row 24: K6, P3, * (K5, P3) twice; rep from * across, end K6.

Rep Rows 1-24 for Garter and Lace pattern.

VEST
BACK

With straight needles, cast on 92{99-113-120} sts.

Work in Lace Rib for 6 rows.

Next (decrease) Row (WS): P2, K1, K2 tog, K1, * P3, K1, K2 tog, K1; rep from * across, end P2 — 79{85-97-103} sts.

Work as established for 3 rows more (working one st less in each purl section next to the lace ribs).

Next (decrease) Row (WS): P2, K1, K2 tog, * P3, K1, K2 tog; rep from * across, end P2 — 66{71-81-86} sts.

Work as established for 3 rows more (working one st less in each purl section next to the lace ribs).

Next (decrease) Row (WS): P2, K2 tog, * P3, K2 tog; rep from * across, end P2 — 53{57-65-69} sts.

Knit 2 rows.

Next Row (RS): Work 3{5-9-3} sts in Garter st, place marker (PM) *(see Markers, page 114)*, work Row 1 of Garter and Lace pattern over 47{47-47-63} sts, PM, work 3{5-9-3} sts in Garter st.

Work in patterns as established until piece above Lace Rib measures 3{3-3^1/$_2$-4}"/7.5{7.5-9-10} cm, end with a WS row.

Armhole Shaping: Bind off 5{5-6-6} sts at the beginning of the next 2 rows — 43{47-53-57} sts.

Work in pattern as established until armhole measures 4{4^1/$_2$-5-5^1/$_2$}"/10{11.5-12.5-14} cm, end with a WS row.

Neck and Shoulder Shaping (RS): K3{5-8-10}, join a second ball of yarn and bind off center 37 sts, knit remaining sts — 3{5-8-10} sts remain each side.

Working both sides at the same time, knit remaining sts on each side.

Bind off remaining 3{5-8-10} sts each side for shoulders.

FRONT
Work same as Back.

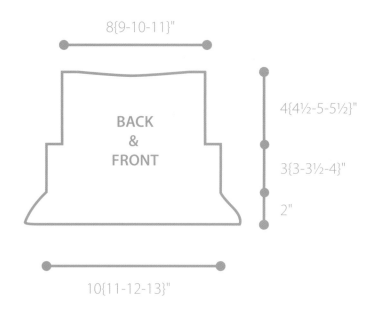

8{9-10-11}"

4{4½-5-5½}"

3{3-3½-4}"

2"

BACK & FRONT

10{11-12-13}"

FINISHING

Sew Front to Back at shoulders.

Front Neckline Trim: With RS facing and straight needles, pick up 34{39-44-49} sts evenly spaced across front neck *(Figs. 14a & b, page 123)*.

Knit 1 row, purl 1 row.

Bind off all sts in knit.

Rep for Back Neckline Trim.

Join trims where they meet at sides of neck.

Armhole Trim: With RS facing and straight needles, pick up 31{36-41-46} sts evenly spaced along entire armhole edge.

Knit 6 rows.

Bind off all sts in knit.

Rep on second armhole.

Sew edges of trim to bound off sts at armhole.

Sew side seams.

BLANKET
UNIT 1

SQUARE 1: With straight needles and A, cast on 47 sts.

Knit WS row.

Next Row (RS): Work Row 1 of Garter and Lace pattern.

Work in pattern as established for 72 rows (3 pattern reps). Piece should measure approximately 9" (23 cm) square.

Bind off all sts in knit.

SQUARE 2: With RS of Square 1 facing, using straight needles and B, pick up 47 sts evenly spaced along RH side of square.

Work as for Square 1.

SQUARE 3: With RS of Square 1 facing, using straight needles and C, pick up 47 sts evenly spaced along LH side of square.

Work as for Square 1.

SQUARE 4: With RS of Square 3 facing, using straight needles and D, pick up 47 sts evenly spaced along RH side of square.

Work as for Square 1.

SQUARE 5: With RS of Square 4 facing, using straight needles and C, pick up 47 sts evenly spaced along RH side of square.

Work as for Square 1.

SQUARE 6: With RS of Square 2 facing, using straight needles and A, pick up 47 sts evenly spaced along LH side of square.

Work as for Square 1.

To complete this Unit 1, sew Squares where they meet: Between Squares 1 and 5, and Squares 5 and 6.

UNIT 2
SQUARE 1: With straight needles and D, cast on 47 sts.

Knit WS row.

Next Row (RS): Work Row 1 of Garter and Lace pattern.

Work in pattern as established for 72 rows (3 pattern reps). Piece should measure approximately 9" (23 cm) square.

Bind off all sts in knit.

SQUARE 2: With RS of Square 1 facing, using straight needles and C, pick up 47 sts evenly spaced along RH side of square.

Work as for Square 1.

SQUARE 3: With RS of Square 1 facing, using straight needles and B, pick up 47 sts evenly spaced along LH side of square.

Work as for Square 1.

SQUARE 4: With RS of Square 3 facing, using straight needles and A, pick up 47 sts evenly spaced along RH side of square.

Work as for Square 1.

SQUARE 5: With RS of Square 4 facing, using straight needles and B, pick up 47 sts evenly spaced along RH side of square.

Work as for Square 1.

SQUARE 6: With RS of Square 2 facing, using straight needles and D, pick up 47 sts evenly spaced along LH side of square.

Work as for Square 1.

To complete this Unit 2, sew Squares where they meet: Between Squares 1 and 5, and Squares 5 and 6.

FINISHING
Sew side with Squares 4, 5 and 6 of Unit 1, to side with Squares 1, 2 and 3 of Unit 2.

Trim for Short Edge (square colors A, B & D): With RS facing, using circular needle and C, pick up 141 sts evenly spaced along short edge.

Knit 9 rows.

Bind off all sts in knit.

Trim for Short Edge (square colors A, B & C): With RS facing, using circular needle and D, pick up 141 sts evenly spaced along short edge.

Knit 9 rows.

Bind off all sts in knit.

Trim for RH Long Edge: With RS facing, using circular needle and A, pick up 200 sts evenly spaced along RH long edge, including trim on short edges.

Knit 9 rows.

Bind off all sts in knit.

Trim for LH Long Edge: With RS facing, using circular needle and B, pick up 200 sts evenly spaced along LH long edge, including trim on short edges.

Knit 9 rows.

Bind off all sts in knit.

PETAL PINK
Cardigan and Blanket

Could any book of baby sweaters be complete without a project in the utmost girlie color? Yet I am equally convinced that this set would be as delightful in a deep violet or a bright emerald green! Or boyish blue— perhaps with baby's first initial in place of the flower. The unusual trellis-like pattern in both cardigan and blanket has large double yarn-over eyelets. The blanket has an interesting cable that shares this openwork. It also has a bold border with distinctive mitered corners. In contrast, areas of smooth Stockinette stitch highlight the textured patterns. A lightweight blend of cotton and cashmere lends a delicacy to these fabrics. The blanket could be worked in a slightly heavier weight of yarn—or the cardigan yarn doubled— for a bolder effect and a somewhat larger size.

SIZES
To fit sizes 6{12-18-24} months
Sample worked in size 12 months.

FINISHED MEASUREMENTS
Cardigan:
  Chest at underarm:
    22$\frac{1}{2}${25-28-30$\frac{1}{2}$}"/
    57{63.5-71-77.5} cm
  Length:
    11$\frac{1}{2}${12-12$\frac{1}{2}$-13}"/
    29{30.5-32-33} cm
  Sleeve width at upper arm:
    11{12-13-14}"/
    28{30.5-33-35.5} cm
Blanket: 25" wide x 28" long
    (63.5 cm x 71 cm)

Size Note: Instructions for Cardigan
are written for size 6 months
with sizes 12, 18 and 24 months
in braces { }. Instructions will be
easier to read if you circle all the
numbers pertaining to your baby's
size. If only one number is given, it
applies to all sizes.

MATERIALS
ROWAN "Cashsoft DK"
(57% Extra Merino Wool, 33%
Acrylic Microfiber, 10% Cashmere;
50 grams/126 yards)
Color #540 (Sky Pink)
  Cardigan: 3{4-5-5} balls
  Blanket: 7 balls
Straight knitting needles,
  sizes 5 (3.75 mm) **and** 6 (4 mm)
  or sizes needed to obtain
  gauge
24" (61 cm) Circular knitting
  needle, size 6 (4 mm)
Stitch holders (for cardigan) - 2
$\frac{5}{8}$" (16 mm) Shell or
  mother-of-pearl buttons - 4
  (for Cardigan)
$\frac{1}{4}$" (7 mm) Button - 1
  (for Cardigan flower)
Cable needle (for Blanket)
Stitch markers (for Blanket)
Tapestry needle

GAUGE
Over Large Eyelet pattern
with size 6 needles:
24 sts and 32 rows = 4" (10 cm)
Take time to save time, check your
gauge.

Techniques used:
• YO *(Fig. 5a, page 117)*
• Bar increase *(Figs. 6a & b, page 118)*
• M1 *(Figs. 7a & b, page 119)*
• K2 tog *(Fig. 8, page 119)*
• SSK *(Figs. 10a-c, page 120)*

PATTERN STITCHES
STOCKINETTE STITCH (St st):
Any number of sts
Knit RS rows, purl WS rows.

LARGE EYELET PATTERN:
Multiple of 8 sts plus 6
Right Twist (RT): K2 tog, leave sts
on needle, then insert RH needle
between 2 sts just knitted tog and
knit the first st again, then slip both
sts from LH needle.
Left Twist (LT): Knit into the back
of the second st, then knit the first
st, and slip both sts off needle tog.

Row 1 (RS): K6, * RT, K6; rep from *
across.
Row 2: Purl across.
Row 3: K5, * K2 tog, YO twice, SSK,
K4; rep from * across, end last rep
K5.
Row 4: Purl across, purling once
into each double YO, letting the
extra loop drop from needle.

Row 5: K4, * K2 tog, K1 **below** into YO space, K1, K1 **below** into YO space, SSK, K2; rep from * across, end last rep K4.

Row 6: P6, * P1 **below** into YO space, P7; rep from * across.

Row 7: K3, * K2 tog, K2, K1 **below** into YO space, K2, SSK; rep from * across, end K3.

Row 8: P6, * P1 **below** into YO space, P7; rep from * across.

Row 9: K2, LT, * K6, LT; rep from * across, end K2.

Row 10: Purl across.

Row 11: K1, K2 tog, YO twice, SSK, * K4, K2 tog, YO twice, SSK; rep from * across, end K1.

Row 12: Purl across, purling once into each double YO, letting the extra loop drop from needle.

Row 13: K2 tog, K1 **below** into YO space, K1, K1 **below** into YO space, SSK, * K2, K2 tog, K1 **below** into YO space, K1, K1 **below** into YO space, SSK; rep from * across.

Row 14: P2, P1 **below** into YO space, * P7, P1 **below** into YO space; rep from * across, end P3.

Row 15: SSK, K1, K1 **below** into YO space, * K2, SSK, K2 tog, K2, K1 **below** into YO space; rep from * across, end K1, K2 tog.

Row 16: P2, P1 **below** into YO space, * P7, P1 **below** into YO space; rep from * across, end P3.

Rep Rows 1-16 for Large Eyelet pattern.

CARDIGAN
BODY

Note: Body is worked in one piece to armholes, then Fronts and Back are worked separately.

With circular needle, cast on 136{152-168-184} sts.

Working back and forth, purl WS row.

Establish Pattern (RS): K1 (St st edge st), work Row 1 of Large Eyelet pattern over 134{150-166-182} sts, end K1 (St st edge st).

Work even until 48 pattern rows are complete (3 reps of pattern), ending with a WS row, piece measures approximately 6" (15 cm).

Knit RS row.

Divide for Armholes (WS): Purl 34{38-42-46} sts and slip these sts onto st holder for Left Front, purl 68{76-84-92} sts and slip these sts onto st holder for Back, then purl remaining 34{39-42-46} sts for Right Front.

Right Front: Work even on 34{38-42-46} sts in St st until armhole measures 4{4^1/$_2$-5-5^1/$_2$}"/ 10{11.5-12.5-14} cm, end with a WS row.

Neck Shaping: Bind off 7{9-10-11} sts at the beginning of the next RS row, then 3 sts at the beginning of the next 3 RS rows — 18{20-23-26} sts remain.

Work even until armhole measures 5^1/$_2${6-6^1/$_2$-7}"/14{15-16.5-18} cm, end with a WS row.

Bind off remaining 18{20-23-26} sts for shoulder.

Left Front: With RS facing, slip sts from Left Front st holder onto size 6 straight needles.
Attach yarn at beginning of RS row at armhole edge.

Work even on 34{38-42-46} sts in St st until armhole measures 4{4^1/$_2$-5-5^1/$_2$}"/10{11.5-12.5-14} cm, end with a RS row, one more row than for Right Front.

Neck Shaping: Bind off 7{9-10-11} sts at the beginning of the next WS row, then 3 sts at the beginning of the next 3 WS rows — 18{20-23-26} sts remain.

Work even until armhole measures 5^1/$_2${6-6^1/$_2$-7}"/14{15-16.5-18} cm, end with a WS row.

Bind off remaining 18{20-23-26} sts for shoulder.

Back: With RS facing, slip sts from Back st holder onto size 6 straight needles.
Attach yarn at beginning of RS row at armhole edge.

Work even on 68{76-84-92} sts in St st until armhole measures 5^1/$_4${5^3/$_4$-6^1/$_4$-6^3/$_4$}"/ 13.5{14.5-16-17} cm, end with a WS row.

Neck Shaping: Mark center 32{36-38-40} sts.
Work to center 32{36-38-40} sts, join a second ball of yarn and bind off center sts, work as established to end — 18{20-23-26} sts remain each side.

Working both sides at the same time, work WS row.

Bind off remaining 18{20-23-26} sts each side for shoulders.

SLEEVE (Make 2)

With size 6 straight needles, cast on 40{48-48-56} sts.

Purl WS row.

Next Row (RS): K1 (St st edge st), work Row 1 of Large Eyelet pattern over 38{46-46-54} sts, end K1 (St st edge st).

Work even until 32 pattern rows are complete (2 reps of pattern), ending with a WS row, piece measures approximately 4" (10 cm).

Next Row (RS): Knit across increasing 26{26-30-28} sts evenly spaced (see Increasing Or Decreasing Evenly Across A Row, page 118) — 66{74-78-84} sts.

Work even in St st until Sleeve measures approximately 8{8½-9-9½}"/ 20.5{21.5-23-24} cm, end with a WS row.

Bind off all sts in knit.

FINISHING

Sew Front to Back at shoulders.
Sew Sleeve seams.
Sew Sleeves into armholes.

Neckline Trim: With RS of Right Front facing and using size 5 straight needles, pick up 17{22-22-23} sts evenly spaced across to shoulder (*Figs. 14a & b, page 123*), 29{31-33-35} sts evenly spaced across to left shoulder, then 17{22-22-23} sts evenly spaced across to Left Front edge — 63{75-77-81} sts.

Knit 3 rows.

Bind off all sts in knit.

Left Front Button Band: With RS facing and using size 5 straight needles, pick up 57{59-61-63} sts evenly spaced along Left Front edge.

Knit 3 rows.

Bind off all sts in knit.

Right Front Buttonhole Band: With RS facing and using size 5 straight needles, pick up 57{59-61-63} sts evenly spaced along Right Front edge.

Buttonhole Row (WS): K2, K2 tog, YO, SSK, (K5, K2 tog, YO, SSK) 3 times, knit to end — 53{55-57-59} sts.

Next Row: Knit each st and (K1, P1) into each YO of the previous row — 57{59-61-63} sts.

Knit WS row.

Bind off all sts in knit.

Sew ⅝" (16 mm) buttons to Button Band opposite buttonholes.

Flower: With size 5 straight needles, cast on 60 sts.

Purl 1 row.

Bind off all sts in knit with size 6 straight needle.

Make 5 small loops, tack in place and sew small button to center.

Sew Flower to Cardigan.

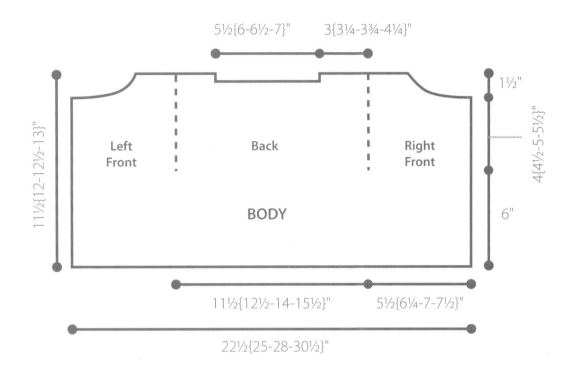

5½{6-6½-7}"   3{3¼-3¾-4¼}"

1½"

Left
Front

Back

Right
Front

4{4½-5-5½}"

11½{12-12½-13}"

BODY

6"

11½{12½-14-15½}"   5½{6¼-7-7½}"

22½{25-28-30½}"

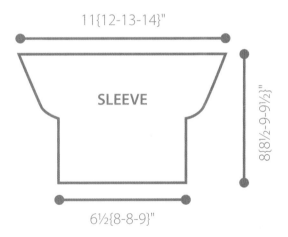

11{12-13-14}"

SLEEVE

8{8½-9-9½}"

6½{8-8-9}"

BLANKET

CABLE PANEL: Panel of 10 sts
Row 1: K2, P6, K2.
Row 2 (RS): P2, K1, K2 tog, YO twice, SSK, K1, P2.
Row 3: K2, P2, (K1, P1) into the double YO, P2, K2.
Row 4: P2, K6, P2.
Row 5: K2, P6, K2.
Row 6: P2, slip next 4 sts onto cn and hold in front, K2, then slip the last 2 sts from cn back to LH needle and knit them, then K2 from cn, P2.
Rows 7-18: Rep Rows 1-4, 3 times.
Rep Rows 1-18 for Cable Panel.

With size 6 needles, cast on 112 sts.

Preparation Row (WS): P 31 sts, place marker (PM) *(see Markers, page 114)*, K2, P6, K2, PM, purl center 30 sts, PM, K2, P6, K2, PM, P 31 sts.

Establish Patterns (RS): K1 (St st edge st), PM, work Row 1 of Large Eyelet pattern over 30 sts, slip marker, work Row 2 of Cable Panel, slip marker, work Row 1 of Large Eyelet pattern over center 30 sts, slip marker, work Row 2 of Cable Panel, slip marker, work Row 1 of Large Eyelet pattern over 30 sts, PM, end K1 (St st edge st).

Work even until Blanket measures 21" (53.5 cm).

Bind off all sts in pattern.

FINISHING

TEXTURED PATTERN: Multiple of 3 sts
Rnds 1-4: Knit around.
Rnds 5-8: * K2, P1; rep from * around.
Rnds 9-12: * K1, P2; rep from * around.
Rep Rnds 1-12 for Textured pattern.

Preparation Rnd: With RS facing and circular needle, starting at corner of cast on edge, pick up 102 sts evenly spaced along cast on edge, PM, pick up 2 sts in corner, PM, pick up 120 sts evenly spaced across long side of Blanket to corner, PM, pick up 2 sts in corner, PM, pick up 102 sts evenly spaced along bound off edge, PM, pick up 2 sts in corner, PM, pick up 120 sts evenly spaced across long edge of Blanket to corner, PM, pick up 2 sts in corner, PM and join — 452 sts.

Establish Patterns: * Work Rnd 1 of Textured pattern over 102 sts, slip marker, K2 corner sts, slip marker, work Rnd 1 of Textured pattern over 120 sts, slip marker, K2 corner sts, slip marker; repeat from * once more.

Increase Rnd: * M1, work next rnd of Textured pattern across to next marker, M1, slip marker, K2 corner sts, slip marker; repeat from * 3 times more — 460 sts.

Note: When working Rnd 5 of Textured pattern, begin to establish pattern right after each marker, even though, due to the increases, it is no longer a multiple of 3 sts. It may be helpful to make a swatch of the Textured pattern, to see how the sts line up.

Working increases in Textured pattern, rep the Increase Rnd until a total of 2 reps of Textured pattern (24 rnds) have been worked.

Bind off all sts, working Rnd 12 of Textured pattern.

Pom-Pom Poncho
A Hooded Pullover Poncho

Instead of a bunting, why not knit a wintertime poncho for Baby, with the added detailing of a warm hood! This is an easy-to-knit future heirloom, made entirely in square pieces, with just a bit of neckline shaping. The ridged knit/purl pattern of Austrian origin is easy to remember and so pleasant to knit. It is deeply textured for warmth and good looks. I chose a luxurious blend of baby alpaca and merino in a timeless earthy brown. For the finishing touches, I used charming buttons and made thick, delightful pom-poms to give some whimsy to the piece. In a heavier yarn, this simple ridged fabric would also make a lovely blanket. Knit it in a firm cotton, and you could fashion it into a simple necessities bag for Mom.

EASY +

SIZES
To fit sizes 6{12-18-24} months
Sample worked in size 12 months.

FINISHED MEASUREMENTS
Width of Back and Front (1¹/₂" trim each side):
   19¹/₂{23-26¹/₂-30}"/
   49.5{58.5-67.5-76} cm
Length: 14¹/₂{14¹/₂-15¹/₂-15¹/₂}"/
   37{37-39.5-39.5} cm

Size Note: Instructions are written for size 6 months with sizes 12, 18 and 24 months in braces { }. Instructions will be easier to read if you circle all the numbers pertaining to your baby's size. If only one number is given, it applies to all sizes.

MATERIALS

   ROWAN "Lima"
(84% Baby Alpaca,
8% Merino Wool, 8% Nylon;
50 grams/109 yards)
   Color #889 (Peru): 5 {6-7-8} balls
Straight knitting needles,
   size 9 (5.5 mm) **or** size
   needed to obtain gauge
16" (40.5 cm) Circular knitting
   needle, size 9 (5.5 mm)
Yarn needle
1" (25 mm) Buttons - 6

GAUGE
Over Ridged pattern
with size 9 needles:
19 sts and 32 rows = 4" (10 cm)
Take time to save time, check your gauge.

PATTERN STITCH
RIDGED PATTERN: Multiple of 16 sts
Rows 1 and 3 (RS): * K5, P 11; rep from * across.
Row 2: * K 11, P5; rep from * across.
Rows 4 and 6: Purl across.
Row 5: Knit across.
Rows 7 and 9: P4, K5, * P 11, K5; rep from * across, end P7.
Row 8: K7, P5, * K 11, P5; rep from * across, end K4.
Rows 10 and 12: Purl across.
Row 11: Knit across.
Rows 13 and 15: P8, K5, * P 11, K5; rep from *across, end P3.
Row 14: K3, P5, * K 11, P5; rep from * across, end K8.
Rows 16 and 18: Purl across.
Row 17: Knit across.
Rows 19 and 21: K1, P 11, * K5, P 11; rep from * across, end K4.
Row 20: P4, K 11, * P5, K 11; rep from * across, end P1.
Row 22: Purl across.
Row 23: Knit across.
Row 24: Purl across.
Rep Rows 1-24 for Ridged pattern.

PONCHO
BODY

Front: With size 9 needles, cast on 80{96-112-128} sts.

Work in Ridged pattern until piece measures 11{11-12-12}"/ 28{28-30.5-30.5} cm, end with a WS row.

Front Neck Shaping (RS): Mark center 10 sts.
Work to center 10 sts, join a second ball of yarn and bind off center sts, work to end — 35{43-51-59} sts remain each side.

Keeping in pattern, working both sides at the same time with separate balls of yarn, bind off 2 sts from each Neck edge, 4 times — 27{35-43-51} sts remain each side.

Work even until piece measures 13{13-14-14}"/ 33{33-35.5-35.5} cm, end with a WS row.

Back: Tie a marker at each end of the next RS row to indicate the shoulder line.

Next Row (RS): Work 27{35-43-51} sts in pattern, cast on 26 sts *(Fig. 1, page 114)*, work remaining 27{35-43-51} sts as established — 80{96-112-128} sts.

Working newly cast on sts into pattern, work even until piece measures 13{13-14-14}"/ 33{33-35.5-35.5} cm from shoulder markers.

Bind off all sts in pattern.

HOOD SIDE (Make 2)
With size 9 needles, cast on 32 sts.

Work in Ridged pattern for 6½" (16.5 cm).

Bind off all sts in pattern.

FINISHING
Front Lower Edge Trim: With RS of Front facing and size 9 needles, pick up 66{80-94-108} sts evenly spaced along cast on edge *(Figs. 14a & b, page 123)*.

Knit WS row. Work 2 rows St st.

Purl RS row. Work 2 rows St st.

Knit WS row. Work 2 rows St st.

Purl RS row.

Bind off all sts in knit on WS.

Back Lower Edge Trim: Rep Front Lower Edge Trim along lower bound off edge of Back.

Left Side Trim: With RS of Body facing and size 9 needles, pick up 152{152-162-162} sts evenly spaced along entire left edge.

Work Trim the same as for lower edge.

Right Side Trim: Rep Left Side Trim along right edge.

Hood: With RS of bound off edge of first Hood Side facing (top of hood) and size 9 needles, pick up 30 sts evenly spaced along bound off edge, then 33 sts evenly spaced along side edge (center back of hood) — 63 sts.

Work Trim the same as for lower edge.

Sew top and one side of second Hood Side to trimmed edges of first Hood Side.

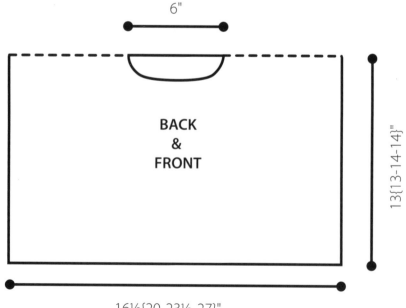

6"

BACK
&
FRONT

13{13-14-14}"

16½{20-23½-27}"

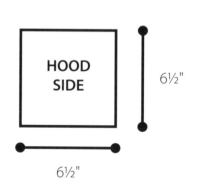

HOOD
SIDE

6½"

6½"

Front of Hood Trim: With RS of front edge facing and size 9 needles, pick up 38 sts evenly spaced along side, 7 sts evenly spaced across hood trim and 38 sts evenly spaced to end — 83 sts.

Knit 1 row, purl 1 row.

Bind off all sts in knit.

Neckline Edging: With RS facing and circular needle, starting at shoulder, pick up 76 sts evenly spaced around neckline.

Turn and knit 2 rnds.

Bind off all sts loosely in knit.

Sew untrimmed edge of hood to neckline edge, along WS ridge formed by picked up sts, leaving a gap of 2" (5 cm) at center front.

Fold poncho so that front and back lower edges meet. Measure 4" (10 cm) down from shoulder fold and sew button through both layers of trim on both sides. Sew another button 4" (10 cm) below first button on both sides. Sew front to back between buttons on each side.

CORD (Make 2)
With size 9 needles, cast on 34 sts.

Bind off all sts in knit.

Make 2 pom-poms *(Figs. 18a-c, page 126)* and sew one to end of each cord. Sew end of cord to base of neckline edging, one on each side of center gap. Sew a button at base of each pom-pom cord at Neck edge.

PRINCESS OF HEARTS
Lace Border Cardigan

No motif is better suited to baby things than that of hearts, and these are worked in lace for a sweet touch. Also sweet is this most unique yarn, a mix of cotton and alpaca, almost as soft and delicate as a baby's skin. What little darling would not look heaven-sent in this detailed raglan cardigan with a pretty yoke, worked in a feather-weight fabric? Your yarn choice is what will make this sweater unique. If you choose a bouncy wool or wool blend, the cardigan would have a more firm quality, rather than the soft drape it has here. For a fluffy confection, choose a lace weight mohair! You can always lengthen or shorten the body or the sleeves to customize this sweater.

SIZES
To fit sizes 6{12-18-24} months
Sample worked in size 12 months.

FINISHED MEASUREMENTS
Chest at underarm, buttoned:
21¹/₂{24-26-28¹/₂}"/
54.5{61-66-72.5} cm
Length: 10¹/₂{11-12¹/₂-13¹/₂}"/
26.5{28-32-34.5} cm
Sleeve width at upper arm:
10" (25.5 cm)

Size Note: Instructions are written
for size 6 months with sizes 12,
18 and 24 months in braces { }.
Instructions will be easier to
read if you circle all the numbers
pertaining to your baby's size. If
only one number is given, it applies
to all sizes.

MATERIALS
MANOS del URUGUAY
"Serena"
(60% Baby Alpaca, 40% Pima
Cotton; 50 grams/170 yards)
Color # 2302 (English):
2{3-3-3} hanks
Straight knitting needles, sizes 4
(3.5 mm) **and** 5 (3.75 mm) **or**
sizes needed to obtain gauge
16" (40.5 cm) **or** 24" (61 cm)
Circular knitting needle, sizes 4
(3.5 mm) **and** 5 (3.75 mm)
Stitch holders - 3
Stitch markers
Tapestry needle
¹/₂" (12 mm) Buttons - 3
¹/₄" (6 mm) **and** ¹³/₁₆" (21 mm)
wide Ribbon - 27" (68.5 cm)
each size

GAUGE
Over Ridge pattern
with size 5 needles:
26 sts and 32 rows = 4" (10 cm)
Take time to save time, check your
gauge.

Techniques used:
• YO *(Fig. 5a, page 117)*
• K2 tog *(Fig. 8, page 119)*
• P2 tog *(Fig. 9, page 119)*
• SSK *(Figs. 10a-c, page 120)*
• Slip 1 as if to **knit**, K2 tog, PSSO
(Figs. 12a & b, page 121)

PATTERN STITCHES
STOCKINETTE STITCH (St st):
Any number of sts
Knit RS rows, purl WS rows.

GARTER STITCH: Any number of
sts
Knit every row.

RIDGE PATTERN: Multiple of
15 sts plus 6
Row 1 (RS): K2, P2, * K 13, P2; rep
from * across to last 2 sts, end K2.
Row 2: Purl across.
Rep Rows 1 and 2 for Ridge pattern.

LACE HEART PATTERN: Multiple
of 15 sts plus 6
Row 1 (RS): K2, P2, * K6, YO, SSK, K5,
P2; rep from * across, end K2.
Row 2 and all other WS rows: Purl
across.
Row 3: K2, P2, * K4, K2 tog, YO, K1,
YO, SSK, K4, P2; rep from * across,
end K2.
Row 5: K2, P2, * K3, K2 tog, YO, K3,
YO, SSK, K3, P2; rep from * across,
end K2.
Row 7: K2, P2, K2, * K2 tog, YO,
K5, YO, SSK, K2, P2, K2; rep from *
across.
Row 9: K2, P2, * K1, K2 tog, YO, K3,
YO, SSK, K2, YO, SSK, K1, P2; rep from
* across, end K2.
Row 11: K2, P2, * K3, YO, slip 1,
K2 tog, PSSO, YO, K1, YO, slip 1,
K2 tog, PSSO, YO, K3, P2; rep from *
across, end K2.
Row 13: K2, P2, * K 13, P2; rep from
* across, end K2.
Row 14: Purl across.
Rep Rows 1-14 for Lace Heart
pattern.

CARDIGAN
BODY

Note: Body is worked in one piece to armholes, then fronts and back are worked separately.

With size 4 circular needle, cast on 141{156-171-186} sts.

Lower Edge Trim: Knit 6 rows.

Change to size 5 circular needle.

Work in Ridge pattern for 4 rows.

Change to Lace Heart pattern and work for 42 rows (3 reps of pattern).

Change back to Ridge pattern and work until piece measures 6½" (16.5 cm), end with a RS row.

Divide for Armholes (WS): Work 30{33-36-39} sts as established and slip these sts onto st holder for Left Front, bind off 10{12-14-16} sts, work as established until there are 61{66-71-76} sts on the right needle and slip these sts onto st holder for Back, bind off 10{12-14-16} sts, work as established across remaining sts for Right Front — 30{33-36-39} sts.

Right Front: Keeping in pattern as established, work even for 4 rows.

Next (decrease) Row (RS): Work to last 3 sts, K2 tog, K1 — 29{32-35-38} sts.

Keeping in pattern, work even for 3 rows more.

Rep decrease row every 4th row 5{6-8-9} times, end with a WS row — 24{26-27-29} sts.

Neck Shaping: Continue to work decrease as established at armhole edge one time more AND AT THE SAME TIME, bind off 5{6-6-7} sts at the beginning of the next 1{3-2-4} RS row(s), then 6{7-7-0} sts at the beginning of the next 3{1-2-0} RS row(s) *(see Zeros, page 114)*.

Left Front: With RS facing, slip 30{33-36-39} sts from Left Front st holder onto size 5 straight needles.
Attach yarn at beginning of RS row at armhole edge.

Work same as for Right Front, reversing all shaping, and beginning neck shaping one row before, on WS row.

Back: With RS facing, slip 61{66-71-76} sts from Back st holder onto size 5 straight needles.
Attach yarn at beginning of RS row at armhole edge.

Keeping in pattern as established, work even for 4 rows.

Next (decrease) Row (RS): K1, SSK, work to last 3 sts, K2 tog, K1 — 59{64-69-74} sts.

Keeping in pattern, work even for 3 rows more.

Rep decrease row every 4th row 6{7-9-10} times, end with a WS row — 47{50-51-54} sts.

Slip remaining sts onto st holder.

SLEEVE (Make 2)

With size 4 straight needles, cast on 66 sts.

Lower Edge Trim: Knit 6 rows.

Change to size 5 straight needles.

Work in Ridge pattern for 4 rows.

Change to Lace Heart pattern and work for 14 rows.

Change back to Ridge pattern and work until piece measures 3½" (9 cm), end with a WS row.

Cap Shaping: Continue in pattern as established and bind off 5{6-7-8} sts at the beginning of the next 2 rows — 56{54-52-50} sts.

Keeping in pattern, work even for 2{4-4-6} rows.

Next (decrease) Row (RS): K1, SSK, work to last 3 sts, K2 tog, K1 — 54{52-50-48} sts.

Rep decrease row every 4th{4th-6th-8th} row 3{7-6-4} times, then every 2nd{0-0-6th} row 7{0-0-1} time(s) — 34{38-38-38} sts.

Slip remaining sts onto st holder.

FINISHING
Steam pieces lightly.
Sew Sleeve seams.
Sew Sleeves into armholes.

Neckline Trim: With RS of Right Front facing and size 4 circular needle, pick up 23{25-27-29} sts evenly spaced across neck edge *(Figs. 14a & b, page 123)*, cut yarn, slip 34{38-38-38} sts from Sleeve st holder onto right point of needle, slip 47{50-51-54} sts from Back st holder onto left point of needle then slip them onto right point, slip 34{38-38-38} sts from Sleeve st holder onto right point of needle, then join yarn and pick up 23{25-27-29} sts evenly spaced across Left Front neck edge — 161{176-181-188} sts.

Purl WS row and decrease 5{12-9-8} sts evenly spaced across *(see Increasing or Decreasing Evenly Across a Row, page 118)* — 156{164-172-180} sts.

Next Row (RS): K4, * P4, K4; rep from * across.

Next (eyelet) Row (WS): P4, * K2, YO, K2 tog, P4; rep from * across.

Work in K4/P4 rib as established until Trim measures $1/2$" (12 mm), end with a WS row.

Next (decrease) Row (RS): K1, K2 tog, K1, * P1, P2 tog, P1, K1, K2 tog, K1; rep from * across — 117{123-129-135} sts.

Next Row (WS): P3, * K3, P3; rep from * across.

Next Row (RS): K1, P1, * SSK, P1, K2 tog, P1; rep from * across, end K1 — 79{83-87-91} sts.

Next Row (WS): * K1, P1; rep from * across.

Bind off all sts in rib.

Left Front Button Band: With RS of Left Front facing and size 4 straight needles, starting at base of Neckline Trim, pick up 60{62-68-74} sts evenly spaced across to lower edge.

Knit 3 rows.

Bind off all sts in knit.

Right Front Buttonhole Band: With RS of Right Front facing and size 4 straight needles, starting at lower edge, pick up 60{62-68-74} sts evenly spaced across to base of Neckline Trim.

Next (buttonhole) Row (WS): K1, K2 tog, YO, SSK, (K8, K2 tog, YO, SSK) twice, knit to end — 57{59-65-71} sts.

Next Row: Knit each st and (K1, P1) into each YO of previous row — 60{62-68-74} sts.

Knit 1 row.

Bind off all sts in knit.

Sew buttons to Button Band opposite buttonholes.

Holding both ribbons together as one, weave ribbon through eyelets at base of Neckline Trim. Tie in bow.

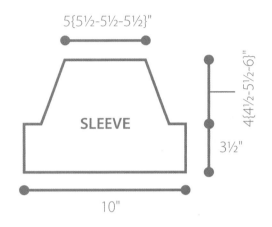

5{5½-5½-5½}"

SLEEVE

4{4½-5½-6}"

3½"

10"

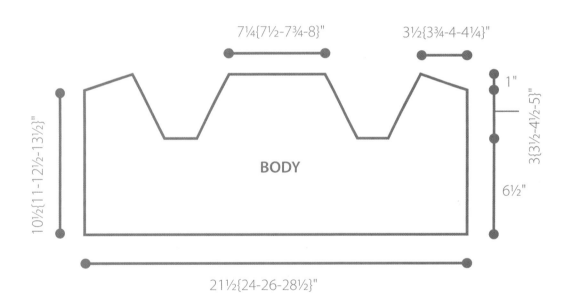

7¼{7½-7¾-8}"

3½{3¾-4-4¼}"

1"

BODY

10½{11-12½-13½}"

3{3½-4½-5}"

6½"

21½{24-26-28½}"

Pumpkin Pie

Lace Cardigan Jumper

This little jumper can be worn elegantly, frock-style, with tights—or sporty as a long top with pants. Any mother will welcome such a versatile sweater knitted in lace patterns. As the patterns decrease, they lend the piece its flared shape. Little sleeves and perfect buttons add detail. The version here is knitted in a blend of soft wool, baby alpaca, and angora for the utmost in posh femininity. For a sportier version, but still heirloom quality, work it in a lightweight pima cotton. The jumper would be sweet without the little sleeves—just simple garter stitch edging at the armholes. Or make the straight sleeves longer for a loose fitting cardigan. If you wanted to make this a short cardigan, you could work the Lace Pattern section to a shorter length.

SIZES
To fit sizes 6{12-18-24} months
Sample worked in size 12 months.

FINISHED MEASUREMENTS
Chest at underarm, buttoned:
 19{21-23-25}"/
 48.5{53.5-58.5-63.5} cm
Length:
 14¹/₂{14¹/₂-15-15¹/₂}"/
 37{37-38-39.5} cm
Sleeve width at upper arm:
 9{10¹/₂-10¹/₂-10¹/₂}"/
 23{26.5-26.5-26.5} cm

Size Note: Instructions are written
for size 6 months with sizes 12,
18 and 24 months in braces { }.
Instructions will be easier to
read if you circle all the numbers
pertaining to your baby's size. If
only one number is given, it applies
to all sizes.

MATERIALS
CLASSIC ELITE "Fresco"
(60% Wool, 30% Baby Alpaca,
 10% Angora; 50 grams/164 yards)
 Color #5385 (Tandori Spice):
 3{4-4-4} hanks
Straight knitting needles, sizes 5
 (3.75 mm) **and** 6 (4 mm) **or**
 sizes needed to obtain gauge
24" (61 cm) Circular knitting
 needle, size 6 (4 mm)
Stitch holders - 2
Stitch markers
Tapestry needle
³/₄" (19 mm) Buttons - 4

GAUGE
Over Lace pattern
with size 6 needles:
25 sts and 31 rows = 4" (10 cm)
Take time to save time, check your
gauge.

Techniques used:
• YO *(Fig. 5a, page 115)*
• K2 tog *(Fig. 8, page 119)*
• P2 tog *(Fig. 9, page 119)*
• SSK *(Figs. 10a-c, page 120)*
• Slip 1 as if to **knit**, K2 tog, PSSO
 (Figs. 12a & b, page 121)

PATTERN STITCHES
STOCKINETTE STITCH (St st):
Any number of sts
Knit RS rows, purl WS rows.

**LACE PATTERN: Multiple of 9 sts
plus 4**
Rows 1 and 3 (WS): Purl across.
Row 2: K3, * YO, K2, SSK, K2 tog, K2,
YO, K1; rep from * across, end K1.
Row 4: K2, * YO, K2, SSK, K2 tog, K2,
YO, K1; rep from * across, end K2.
Rep Rows 1-4 for Lace pattern.

LACE BORDER PATTERN:
Multiple of 17 sts plus 2
Row 1 (RS): K2, * K5, K2 tog, YO, K1,
YO, SSK, K7; rep from * across.
Row 2 and all WS rows: Purl across.
Row 3: K2, * K4, K2 tog, YO, K3, YO,
SSK, K6; rep from * across.
Row 5: K2, * K3, (K2 tog, YO) twice,
K1, (YO, SSK) twice, K5; rep from *
across.
Row 7: K2, * K2, (K2 tog, YO) twice,
K3, (YO, SSK) twice, K4; rep from *
across.
Row 9: K2, * K1, (K2 tog, YO) 3 times,
K1, (YO, SSK) 3 times, K3; rep from *
across.
Row 11: K2, * (K2 tog, YO) 3 times,
K3, (YO, SSK) 3 times, K2; rep from *
across.
Row 13: K2, * K1, (K2 tog, YO) twice,
K5, (YO, SSK) twice, K3; rep from *
across.
Row 15: K2, * K2, K2 tog, YO, K3,
YO, SSK, K2, YO, SSK, K4; rep from *
across.
Row 17: K2, * K3, YO, SSK, K5,
K2 tog, YO, K5; rep from * across.
Row 19: K2, * K4, YO, SSK, K3,
K2 tog, YO, K6; rep from * across.
Row 21: K2, * K5, YO, SSK, K1,
K2 tog, YO, K7; rep from * across.
Row 23: K2, * K6, YO, slip 1, K2 tog,
PSSO, YO, K8; rep from * across.
Row 24: Purl across.

CARDIGAN
BODY

Note: Body is worked in one piece to armholes, then fronts and back are worked separately.

With size 6 circular needle, cast on 166{184-202-220} sts.

Working back and forth, knit RS row.

Establish Pattern (WS): Begin Lace pattern and work until piece measures 2¹/₂" (6.5 cm), ending with a WS row.

Knit RS row, decreasing 11{12-13-14} sts evenly spaced across *(see Increasing or Decreasing Evenly Across a Row, page 118)* — 155{172-189-206} sts.

Purl WS row.

Change to Lace Border pattern and work until 24 rows are complete.

Knit RS row.

Purl WS row, decreasing 25{24-32-31} sts evenly spaced across — 130{148-157-175} sts.

Beginning with Row 2 of pattern, continue in Lace pattern until piece measures 8¹/₂" (21.5 cm), ending with a RS row.

Purl WS row, decreasing 17{23-20-24} sts evenly spaced across — 113{125-137-151} sts.

Work even in St st for 7 rows, ending with a RS row.

Divide for Armholes (WS): Purl 28{31-34-38} sts and slip these sts onto st holder for Left Front, purl 57{63-69-75} sts and slip these sts onto st holder for Back, then purl remaining 28{31-34-38} sts for Right Front.

Right Front: Work in St st on 28{31-34-38} sts for 2 rows, ending with a WS row.

Establish Patterns (RS): Work 3{4-5-7} sts in St st (front edge), place marker (PM) *(see Markers, page 114)*, work Row 1 of Lace Border pattern over 19 sts, work remaining 6{8-10-12} sts in St st (armhole edge).

Continue in patterns until 24 rows of Lace Border pattern are complete.

Change to St st and work until armhole measures 3¹/₂{3¹/₂-4-4¹/₂}"/9{9-10-11.5} cm, end with a WS row.

Neck Shaping: Bind off 6{6-6-7} sts at the beginning of the next RS row, then bind off 3 sts at the beginning of the next 3 RS rows — 13{16-19-22} sts.

Work even in St st until armhole measures 5{5-5¹/₂-6}"/ 12.5{12.5-14-15} cm, end with a WS row.

Bind off remaining 13{16-19-22} sts for shoulder.

Left Front: With RS facing, slip 28{31-34-38} sts from Left Front st holder onto size 6 straight needles.
Attach yarn at beginning of RS row at armhole edge.

Work in St st for 2 rows.

Establish Patterns (RS): Work 6{8-10-12} sts in St st (armhole edge), PM, work Row 1 of Lace Border pattern over 19 sts, work remaining 3{4-5-7} sts in St st (front edge).

Work same as for Right Front, reversing shaping by beginning Neck Shaping one row later, on a WS row.

Back: With RS facing, slip 57{63-69-75} sts from Back st holder onto size 6 straight needles.
Attach yarn at beginning of RS row at armhole edge.

Work in St st for 2 rows.

Establish Patterns (RS): Work 2{5-8-11} sts in St st, PM, work Row 1 of Lace Border pattern over 53 sts, PM, work remaining 2{5-8-11} sts in St st.

Continue in patterns until 24 rows of Lace Border pattern are complete.

Change to St st and work until armhole depth is 2 rows less than Fronts to shoulder, ending with a WS row.

Neck Shaping: Mark center 31 sts. Knit to center 31 sts, join a second ball of yarn and bind off center sts, knit to end — 13{16-19-22} sts remain each side.

Working both sides at the same time, purl WS row.

Bind off remaining 13{16-19-22} sts each side for shoulders.

SLEEVE (Make 2)
With size 6 straight needles, cast on 58{67-67-67} sts.

Knit RS row.

Work in Lace pattern until Sleeve measures 2" (5 cm), end with a WS row.

Bind off all sts in knit.

FINISHING
Sew Fronts to Back at shoulders.
Sew Sleeve seams.
Sew Sleeves into armholes.

Neckline Trim: With RS of Right Front facing and size 5 straight needles, pick up 16{18-20-22} sts evenly spaced across to right shoulder *(Figs. 14a & b, page 123)*, 30{34-38-42} sts evenly spaced across to left shoulder, then 16{18-20-22} sts evenly spaced across to Left Front edge — 62{70-78-86} sts.

Knit 3 rows.

Bind off all sts in knit.

Left Front Button Band: With RS facing and size 5 straight needles, pick up 72{72-74-76} sts evenly spaced along Left Front edge.

Knit 3 rows.

Bind off all sts in knit.

Right Front Buttonhole Band: With RS facing and size 5 straight needles, pick up 72{72-74-76} sts evenly spaced along Right Front edge.

Next (buttonhole) Row (WS): K3, make a 3-st buttonhole (by binding off 3 sts and casting on 3 sts while working bind off row), (K 12, make a 3-st buttonhole) 3 times, knit to end.

Knit 2 rows.

Bind off all sts in knit.

Sew buttons to Button Band opposite buttonholes.

SLEEVE

2"

9{10½-10½-10½}"

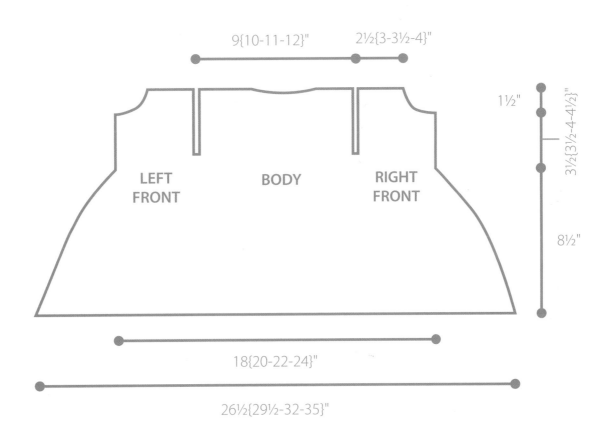

9{10-11-12}"   2½{3-3½-4}"

1½"

3½{3½-4-4½}"

8½"

LEFT
FRONT

BODY

RIGHT
FRONT

18{20-22-24}"

26½{29½-32-35}"

SEA SHELLS
Cotton Striped Pullover

For this boxy, deep-textured, easy-to-knit summer baby sweater, I used the softest of cotton yarns in bright sun-drenched shades. But why not consider this pattern to make a warm and cozy winter pullover? Just choose a wool or wool blend yarn of the same gauge. For a cool weather version, you might want to work a stretch of ribbing over the neckline stitches at the end, on both front and back, instead of the simple neckline shown here. When finishing the sweater, simply sew the ribbed areas at the sides, and fold over like a turtleneck. I am sure this sweater would be delightful worked in a solid version, or in two colors, should you wish.

SIZES
To fit sizes 6{12-18-24} months
Sample worked in size 24 months.

FINISHED MEASUREMENTS
Chest at underarm:
  24{26-28-30}"/
  61{66-71-76} cm
Length:
  10{10-11½-11½}"/
  25.5{25.5-29-29} cm
Sleeve width at upper arm:
  11{12-13-14}"/
  28{30.5-33-35.5} cm

Size Note: Instructions are written for size 6 months with sizes 12, 18 and 24 months in braces { }. Instructions will be easier to read if you circle all the numbers pertaining to your baby's size. If only one number is given, it applies to all sizes.

MATERIALS
BLUE SKY ALPACA
"Worsted Cotton"
(100% Organic Cotton;
100 grams/150 yards) in colors:
  A #604 (Aloe): 1{2-2-2} hank(s)
  B #614 (Drift): 1{2-2-2} hank(s)
  C #638 (Dandelion):
    1{2-2-2} hank(s)
Straight knitting needles, sizes 7
  (4.5 mm) **and** 8 (5 mm) **or** sizes
  needed to obtain gauge
Stitch holders - 4
Stitch markers
Yarn needle

GAUGE
Over St st with size 8 needles:
16 sts and 24 rows = 4" (10 cm)
Over Shell pattern
with size 8 needles:
Panel of 33 sts = 8" (20.5 cm)
Take time to save time, check your gauge.

Techniques used:
• YO *(Fig. 5a, page 117)*
• M1 *(Figs. 7a & b, page 119)*
• K2 tog *(Fig. 8, page 119)*
• SSK *(Figs. 10a-c, page 120)*
• Slip 1 as if to **knit**, K2 tog, PSSO *(Figs. 12a & b, page 121)*

PATTERN STITCHES
GARTER STITCH: Any number of sts
Knit every row.

STOCKINETTE STITCH (St st): Any number of sts
Knit RS rows, purl WS rows.

SHELL PANEL: Panel of 33 sts
Row 1 (RS): K1, * YO, K1, (P1, K1) 7 times, YO, K1; rep from * once more — 37 sts.
Row 2: K1, * P2, K1, (P1, K1) 6 times, P2, K1; rep from * once more.
Row 3: K1, * K1, YO, K1, (P1, K1) 7 times, YO, K2; rep from * once more — 41 sts.
Row 4: K1, * K1, P2, K1, (P1, K1) 6 times, P2, K2; rep from * once more.
Row 5: K1, * K2, YO, K1, (P1, K1) 7 times, YO, K3; rep from * once more — 45 sts.
Row 6: K1, * K2, P2, K1, (P1, K1) 6 times, P2, K3; rep from * once more.
Row 7: K1, * K3, YO, K1, (P1, K1) 7 times, YO, K4; rep from * once more — 49 sts.
Row 8: K1, * K3, P2, K1, (P1, K1) 6 times, P2, K4; rep from * once more.
Row 9: K1, * K4, SSK 3 times, slip 1, K2 tog, PSSO, K2 tog 3 times, K5; rep from * once more — 33 sts.
Row 10: Change to next color and purl across.
Rep Rows 1-10 for Shell Panel.

Shell Pattern Color Sequence:
When working Shell Panel, change colors on Row 10 of every pattern rep as follows:
* With A, work first 9 rows, then switch to B for Row 10.
Continue with B for 9 rows more, then switch to C for Row 10.
Continue with C for 9 rows more, then switch to A for Row 10.
Rep from * for Color Sequence; AND at the same time, work Garter st and St st sections at sides of Shell Panel in same color sequence.

PULLOVER
BACK
With size 8 needles and A, cast on 49{53-57-61} sts.

Establish Patterns (RS): Work in Garter st over 8{10-12-14} sts, place marker (PM) *(see Markers, page 114)*, work Row 1 of Shell Panel (in Color sequence as described) over center 33 sts, PM, work in Garter st over 8{10-12-14} sts.

Work even for 5 rows more, end with a WS row.

Change Pattern at Sides (RS): Work 8{10-12-14} sts in St st, slip marker, continue Shell Panel over center sts, slip marker, work 8{10-12-14} sts in St st.

Keeping sides in St st, work even as established until 6{6-7-7} stripes of Shell Panel have been completed.

Change to size 7 needles and purl 2 rows.

Neck and Shoulder Shaping (RS): K 11{13-15-17} sts, bind off center 27 sts in purl, knit remaining sts — 11{13-15-17} sts remain each side.

Place shoulder sts onto st holders.

FRONT
Work same as for Back.

SLEEVE (Make 2)
With size 8 needles and A, cast on 37{37-39-43} sts.

Establish Patterns (RS): Work in Garter st over 2{2-3-5} sts, PM, work Row 1 of Shell Panel (in Color sequence as described) over center 33 sts, PM, work in Garter st over 2{2-3-5} sts.

Work even for 5 rows more, end with a WS row.

Increase and Change Pattern at Sides (RS): K2, M1, K 0{0-1-3} *(see Zeros, page 114)*, slip marker, continue Shell Panel over center sts, slip marker, K 0{0-1-3}, M1, end K2 — 39{39-41-45} sts.

Keeping in St st at sides and working increases into St st, rep increase row every 10th{6th-4th-4th} row, 3{5-6-6} times more — 45{49-53-57} sts.

Work even as established until 4 stripes of Shell Panel are complete (do not change yarn color on last Row 10).
Piece measures approximately 6½" (16.5 cm).

With A bind off all sts in knit.

FINISHING
With WS facing, join shoulders using corresponding color and 3-needle bind off *(Fig. 15, page 124)*, slipping shoulder sts onto size 8 needles and binding off with a size 7 needle.

Mark 5½{6-6½-7}"/ 14{15-16.5-18} cm down from shoulder on Front and Back.

Sew Sleeves between markers. Sew side and Sleeve seams.

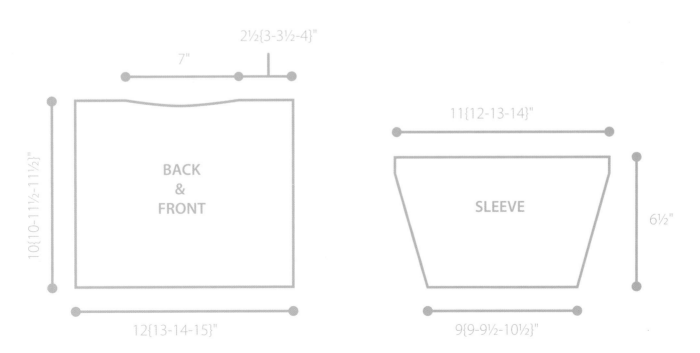

2½{3-3½-4}"

7"

10{10-11½-11½}"

BACK
&
FRONT

12{13-14-15}"

11{12-13-14}"

SLEEVE

6½"

9{9-9½-10½}"

SEED & CABLES
Cardigan, Pants, Hat, & Blanket

As a New Englander, I know the need for a warm set of wrappings for baby! In my neighborhood, mothers stroll their babies down a tree-lined park path in even the coldest months. These fresh-air babies were my inspiration for this bold cardigan, chunky pants, little hat and cozy stroller blanket. I chose a smooth, traditional 100% wool in the softest gold shade. All of the pieces of this ensemble feature simple check patterns with plenty of seed-like detail. Notice that I used wooden toggle buttons—even at the tip of the hat!—for an outdoorsy look. If I were to make this set again, I might work each piece, including the squares of the blanket, in different colors for a bold nursery effect.

SIZES

To fit sizes 6{12-18-24} months
Sample worked in size 12 months.

FINISHED MEASUREMENTS

Cardigan:
  Chest at underarm, including
  1" (2.5 cm) front band:
    23$\frac{1}{2}${25-28-31$\frac{1}{2}$}"/
    59.5{63.5-71-80} cm
  Length: 12{13-14-15}"/
    30.5{33-35.5-38} cm
  Sleeve width at upper arm:
    10$\frac{1}{2}${12-12$\frac{1}{2}$-14}"/
    26.5{30.5-32-35.5} cm
Pants:
  Waist: 22{24-25-26}"/
    56{61-63.5-66} cm
  Length: 13{14-15-16}"/
    33{35.5-38-40.5} cm
Blanket: 30" x 30" (76 cm x 76 cm)

Size Note: Instructions for Cardigan and Pants are written for size 6 months with sizes 12, 18 and 24 months in braces { }. Instructions will be easier to read if you circle all the numbers pertaining to your baby's size. If only one number is given, it applies to all sizes.

MATERIALS

ROWAN "Pure Wool Aran" **(MEDIUM 4)**
(100% Superwash Wool;
100 grams/186 yards)
  Color #687 (Buttermilk)
Cardigan/Pants/Hat/Socks set:
  4{5-6-7} balls
Blanket: 7 balls
Straight knitting needles,
  size 7 (4.5 mm) **or** size needed
  to obtain gauge
24" (61 cm) Circular knitting
  needle, size 7 (4.5 mm)
Crochet hook, size H (5 mm)
  (for Pants)
Cable needle
Stitch holders - 2
Stitch markers
Yarn needle
1" (25 mm) Toggle buttons - 4
  (for Cardigan & Hat)

GAUGE

Over Seed Check pattern
with size 7 needles:
20 sts and 32 rows = 4" (10 cm)
Over Textured pattern
with size 7 needles:
20 sts and 32 rows = 4" (10 cm)
Take time to save time, check your gauge.

Techniques used:
• YO *(Fig. 5c, page 117)*
• M1 *(Figs. 7a & b, page 119)*
• K2 tog *(Fig. 8, page 119)*
• P2 tog *(Fig. 9, page 119)*
• SSK *(Figs. 10a-c, page 120)*

PATTERN STITCHES

STOCKINETTE STITCH (St st):
Any number of sts
Knit RS rows, purl WS rows.

CABLE PANEL: Panel of 12 sts
Back Cross (BC): Slip 2 sts onto cn and hold in back, K2, K2 from cn.
Front Cross (FC): Slip 2 sts onto cn and hold in front, K2, K2 from cn.

Rows 1 and 3 (RS): P2, K8, P2.
Row 2 and all other WS rows: K2, P8, K2.
Row 5: P2, BC, FC, P2.
Row 6: K2, P8, K2.
Rep Rows 1-6 for Cable Panel.

SEED CHECK PATTERN: Multiple of 8 sts plus 3
Row 1 (RS): Knit across.
Row 2: Purl across.
Row 3: K3, * P2, K1, P2, K3; rep from * across.
Row 4: P3, * K1, (P1, K1) 2 times, P3; rep from * across.
Row 5: K3, * P2, K1, P2, K3; rep from * across.
Row 6: P3, * K1, (P1, K1) 2 times, P3; rep from * across.
Row 7: Knit across.
Row 8: Purl across.
Row 9: P1, K1, * P2, K3, P2, K1; rep from * across, end P1.
Row 10: P1, K1, P1, * K1, P3, (K1, P1) 2 times; rep from * across.
Row 11: P1, K1, * P2, K3, P2, K1; rep from *across, end P1.
Row 12: P1, K1, P1, * K1, P3, (K1, P1) 2 times; rep from * across.
Rep Rows 1-12 for Seed Check pattern.

TEXTURED PATTERN: Odd number of sts

Note: The rib stripes, 2 rows each, stagger over each other every 4 rows: They do not line up. So when you increase, be sure to keep in pattern.

Row 1 (RS): Knit across.
Row 2: Purl across.
Row 3: K1, * P1, K1; rep from * across.
Row 4: P1, * K1, P1; rep from * across.
Row 5: Knit across.
Row 6: Purl across.
Row 7: P1, * K1, P1; rep from * across.
Row 8: K1, * P1, K1; rep from * across.
Rep Rows 1-8 for Textured pattern.

DOUBLE MOSS STITCH: Multiple of 4 sts
Row 1 (WS): * K2, P2; rep from * across.
Row 2: * K2, P2; rep from * across.
Row 3: * P2, K2; rep from * across.
Row 4: * P2, K2; rep from * across.
Rep Rows 1-4 for Double Moss st.

SEED TRIM: Even number of sts
Row 1 (WS): Knit across.
Row 2: Knit across.
Rows 3-5: * K1, P1; rep from * across.
Row 6: Knit across.

CARDIGAN
BODY

Note: Body is worked in one piece to armholes, then Fronts and Back are worked separately.

With circular needle, cast on 121{129-145-161} sts.

Work back and forth.

Establish Patterns (RS): K3 (St st edge sts), place marker (PM) *(see Markers, page 114)*, work Row 1 of Cable Panel over 12 sts, work Row 1 of Seed Check pattern over 91{99-115-131} sts, work Row 1 of Cable Panel over 12 sts, PM, end K3 (St st edge sts).

Work even until piece measures 6$\frac{1}{2}${7-7$\frac{1}{2}$-8}"/16.5{18-19-20.5} cm, end with a RS row.

Divide for Armholes (WS): P3, slip marker, work Cable Panel over 12 sts, work 18{20-24-28} sts as established, then slip these 33{35-39-43} sts onto st holder for Left Front, work 55{59-67-75} sts as established and slip these sts onto st holder for Back, then work 18{20-24-28} sts as established, work Cable Panel over 12 sts, slip marker, end P3.

Right Front: Work even in patterns as established on 33{35-39-43} sts until armhole measures 4{4$\frac{1}{2}$-5-5$\frac{1}{2}$}"/ 10{11.5-12.5-14} cm, end with a WS row.

Neck Shaping: Keeping in pattern, bind off 12{12-13-14} sts at the beginning of the next RS row, then 2 sts at the beginning of the next 4 RS rows until armhole measures 5$\frac{1}{2}${6-6$\frac{1}{2}$-7}"/14{15-16.5-18} cm, end with a RS row — 13{15-18-21} sts.

Shoulder Shaping: Bind off 5{5-6-7} sts at the beginning of the next 1{3-3-3} WS row(s), then 4{0-0-0} sts at the beginning of the next 2 WS rows *(see Zeros, page 114)*.

Left Front: With RS facing, slip 33{35-39-43} sts from Left Front st holder onto straight needles. Attach yarn at beginning of RS row at armhole edge.

Work even in patterns as established until armhole measures 4{4$\frac{1}{2}$-5-5$\frac{1}{2}$}"/ 10{11.5-12.5-14} cm, end with a RS row, one more row than for Right Front.

Neck Shaping: Keeping in pattern, bind off 12{12-13-14} sts at the beginning of the next WS row, then 2 sts at the beginning of the next 4 WS rows until armhole measures 5$\frac{1}{2}${6-6$\frac{1}{2}$-7}"/14{15-16.5-18} cm, end with a WS row — 13{15-18-21} sts.

Shoulder Shaping: Bind off 5{5-6-7} sts at the beginning of the next 1{3-3-3} RS row(s), then 4{0-0-0} sts at the beginning of the next 2 RS rows.

Back: With RS facing, slip 55{59-67-75} sts from Back st holder onto straight needles Attach yarn at beginning of RS row at armhole edge.

Work even in patterns as established until armholes measure 5$\frac{1}{2}${6-6$\frac{1}{2}$-7}"/ 14{15-16.5-18} cm, end with a WS row.

Neck and Shoulder Shaping: Mark center 9{9-11-13} sts. Bind off 5{5-6-7} sts, work to center 9{9-11-13} sts, join a second ball of yarn and bind off center sts, work to end.

Working both sides at the same time, bind off 5{5-6-7} sts at the beginning of the next 1{5-5-5} shoulder edge(s), then 4{0-0-0} sts at the beginning of the next 4 shoulder edges, AND AT THE SAME TIME, bind off 5 sts from each Neck edge twice.

SLEEVE (Make 2)

With straight needles, cast on 39{39-47-47} sts.

Establish Patterns (RS): K2 (St st edge sts), work Row 1 of Seed Check pattern over 35{35-43-43} sts, end K2 (St st edge sts).

Work even for 5 rows more, end with a WS row.

Next (increase) Row (RS): K2, M1, work in pattern as established to last 2 sts, M1, end K2 — 41{41-49-49} sts.

Working increases into Seed Check pattern, rep increase row every 4th{4th-6th-6th} row for a total of 9{12-10-13} increases each side — 57{63-67-73} sts.

Work even until Sleeve measures 7$\frac{1}{2}${8$\frac{1}{2}$-10-11}"/ 19{21.5-25.5-28} cm, end with a WS row.

Bind off all sts in pattern.

Sleeve Trim: With RS facing and straight needles, pick up 37{37-41-41} sts evenly spaced along cast on edge (*Figs. 14a & b, page 123*).

Knit WS row, purl RS row.

Bind off all sts in knit.

FINISHING

Sew Fronts to Back at shoulders.
Sew Sleeve seams.
Sew Sleeves into armholes.

Lower Edge Trim: With RS facing and circular needle, beginning at lower Left Front, pick up 2 sts to starting of Cable Panel, pick up 8 sts along Cable Panel, then pick up one st in every cast on st along lower edge to Cable Panel on Right Front, pick up 8 sts along Cable Panel, then 2 sts to end — 111{119-135-151} sts.

Knit WS row, purl RS row.

Bind off all sts in knit.

Left Button Band (for boy, work on Right Front): With RS facing and straight needles, pick up 62{68-74-80} sts evenly spaced along edge.

Work Rows 1-6 of Seed Trim.

Bind off all sts in knit.

Right Buttonhole Band (for boy, work on Left Front): With RS facing and straight needles, pick up 62{68-74-80} sts evenly spaced along edge.

Row 1 (WS): Knit across.

Girl's Buttonhole Row (RS): K 20{26-32-38}, make 5-st buttonhole (by binding off 5 sts and casting on 5 sts while working bind off), (K 12, work 5-st buttonhole) 2 times, knit to end.

Boy's Buttonhole Row (RS): K3, make 5-st buttonhole (by binding off 5 sts and casting on 5 sts while working bind off), (K 12, work 5-st buttonhole) 2 times, knit to end.

Work Rows 3-6 of Seed Trim.

Bind off all sts in knit.

Neckline Trim: With RS facing and circular needle, starting at edge of Trim, pick up 30{30-31-32} sts evenly spaced to right shoulder, 38{38-40-42} sts evenly spaced to left shoulder, then 30{30-31-32} sts evenly spaced to Left Front edge — 98{98-102-106} sts.

Next Row (WS): P2, * K2, P2; rep from * across.

Work in rib as established for $\frac{1}{2}$" (12 mm).

Bind off all sts in rib.

Sew buttons to Button Band opposite buttonholes.

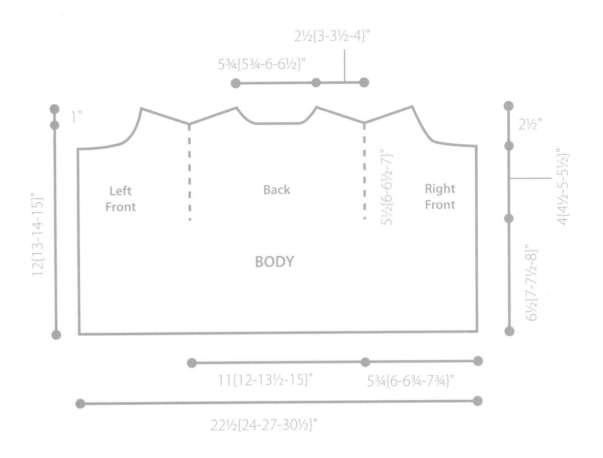

2½{3-3½-4}"

5¾{5¾-6-6½}"

1"

12{13-14-15}"

Left
Front

Back

Right
Front

2½"

4{4½-5-5½}"

5½{6-6½-7}"

BODY

6½{7-7½-8}"

11{12-13½-15}"

5¾{6-6¾-7¾}"

22½{24-27-30½}"

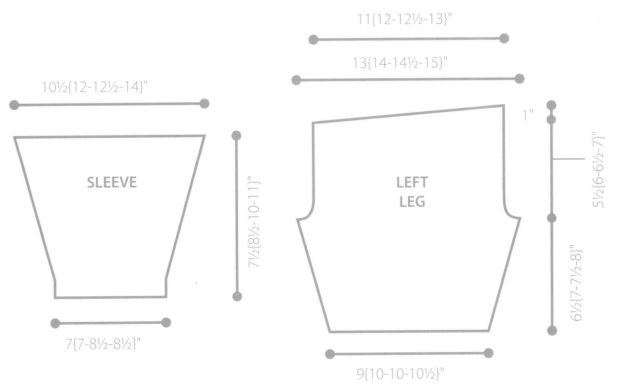

11{12-12½-13}"

13{14-14½-15}"

10½{12-12½-14}"

SLEEVE

7½{8½-10-11}"

LEFT
LEG

1"

5½{6-6½-7}"

6½{7-7½-8}"

7{7-8½-8½}"

9{10-10-10½}"

PANTS

LEFT LEG

With straight needles,
cast on 50{54-54-58} sts.

Establish Patterns (RS):
K2 (St st edge sts), PM, work
Row 1 of Textured pattern over
17{19-19-21} sts, PM, work Row 1
of Cable Panel over center 12 sts,
PM, work Row 1 of Textured pattern
over 17{19-19-21} sts, PM, end
K2 (St st edge sts).

Work even in established patterns
for 7 rows more, end with a WS row.

Next (increase) Row (RS): K2, slip
marker, M1, work as established
to last 2 sts, M1, slip marker, K2 —
52{56-56-60} sts.

Working increases into Textured
pattern, rep increase row every
4th row 9{10-11-10} times more —
70{76-78-80} sts.

Work even until piece measures
6¹/₂{7-7¹/₂-8}"/16.5{18-19-20.5} cm,
end with a WS row.

Note: Tie a yarn marker at the center
of the next crotch row.

Shape Crotch: Keeping in Textured
pattern as established, bind off 3 sts
at the beginning of the next 2 rows,
then bind off 2 sts at the beginning
of the next 2{4-2-2} rows, then
0{0-1-0} st(s) at the beginning of the
next 2 rows — 60{62-66-70} sts.

Next Row (RS): K2 (St st edge sts),
PM, continue Textured pattern as
established over 22{23-25-27} sts,
continue Cable Panel over center
12 sts, slip marker, continue
Textured pattern as established
over 22{23-25-27} sts, PM, end K2
(St st edge sts).

Work as established until
piece measures 5¹/₂{6-6¹/₂-7}"/
14{15-16.5-18} cm from marker,
12{13-14-15}"/30.5{33-35.5-38} cm
total length from beginning, end
with a RS row.

Waist Shaping: Continue in patterns
and bind off 14 sts at the beginning
of the next 0{1-3-5} WS row(s), then
12 sts at the beginning of the next
5{4-2-0} WS rows.

RIGHT LEG

Work same as for Left Leg,
beginning Waist Shaping one row
sooner, on a RS row.

FINISHING

Lower Leg Edge: With RS facing
and straight needles, pick up
46{50-50-54} sts evenly spaced
along cast on edge.

Work Rows 1-6 of Seed Trim.

Bind off all sts in knit.

Rep for second Leg.

Sew Leg and crotch seams.

Waistline Rib: With RS facing
and circular needle, starting
at right Cable Panel, pick up
120{128-136-144} sts evenly
spaced around waistline of
pants. Join and PM for beg of rnd.

Next Rnd: * P2, K2; rep from *
around.

Work in established rib for 2 rnds
more.

Next (eyelet) Rnd: * P2, K2, YO,
P2 tog, K2; rep from * around.

Work in established rib until Rib
measures 1¹/₂" (4 cm).

Bind off all sts in rib.

Cord: With crochet hook, make a
chain 34{36-38-40}"/
86.5{91.5-96.5-101.5} cm long
(Fig. 19, page 127).

Slip st in second chain from hook
(Fig. 20, page 127) and in each
chain across.

Cut yarn and fasten off.

Beginning at center front, thread
cord through eyelet rnd of Pants.

HAT

With straight needles, cast on 71 sts.

Work in Textured pattern for 4" (10 cm), end with a WS row, decreasing one st on last row — 70 sts.

Shape Crown (RS): K1, * SSK, work 15 sts in Textured pattern; rep from * across, end K1 — 66 sts.

Work WS row.

Next (decrease) Row (RS): K1, * SSK, work 14 sts in Textured pattern; rep from * across, end K1 — 62 sts.

Work WS row.

Continue to decrease every RS row as established until there are 54 sts, ending with a WS row.

Next (decrease) Row (RS): K1, * SSK, work 4 sts in Textured pattern, SSK, work 5 sts in Textured pattern; rep from * across, end K1 — 46 sts.

Work WS row.

Next (decrease) Row (RS): K1, * SSK, work 3 sts in Textured pattern, SSK, work 4 sts in pattern; rep from * across, end K1 — 38 sts.

Work WS row.

Continue to decrease as established until there are 14 sts, ending with a WS row.

Next (decrease) Row (RS): * K1, SSK; rep from * across, end K2 — 10 sts.

Work WS row.

Next (decrease) Row (RS): K1, SSK 4 times, end K1 — 6 sts.

Cut yarn and thread yarn through the remaining 6 sts.

Sew side seam.

Decoration (Make 2): With straight needles, cast on 30 sts.

Purl 1 row.

Next Row: At the same time as binding off, (K1, K2 tog) firmly across row.

Sew both at top of Hat, with a toggle button.

BLANKET

Note: The blanket is made up of 4 square blocks (2 different blocks, each worked twice).

BLOCK #1 (Make 2)

With straight needles, cast on 79 sts.

Establish Patterns (RS): K1 (St st edge st), PM, work Row 1 of Textured pattern across 17 sts, PM, work Row 1 of Cable Panel over 12 sts, PM, work Row 1 of Seed Check pattern over center 19 sts, PM, work Row 1 of Cable Panel over 12 sts, PM, work Row 1 of Textured pattern over 17 sts, PM, K1 (St st edge st).

Work even in established patterns until Block is approximately square in size: Measure how wide the piece is, and then knit to approximately that same length, binding off on a RS row.

BLOCK #2 (Make 2)

With straight needles, cast on 79 sts.

Establish Patterns (RS): K1 (St st edge st), PM, work Row 1 of Seed Check pattern over 11 sts, PM, work Row 1 of Cable Panel over 12 sts, PM, work Row 1 of Textured pattern over center 31 sts, PM, work Row 1 of Cable Panel over 12 sts, PM, work Row 1 of Seed Check pattern over 11 sts, PM, K1 (St st edge st).

Work even in established patterns until Block is square in size: This should be approximately the same number of rows as Block #1, binding off on a RS row.

FINISHING

Sew Blocks together as follows:
Sew the cast on edge of first Block #2 to the side of first Block #1. Then sew the cast on edge of second Block #1 to the side edge of the first Block #2 to form an "L" shape.
Sew the cast on edge of the second Block #2 to the side edge of the second Block #1, join this last Block #2 to the first Block #1 on the last unconnected edge, forming the square.

Work Edging as follows: With RS facing and circular needle, pick up 136 sts evenly spaced along one side (68 sts for each square).

Work in Double Moss st for 2½" (6.5 cm), end with a RS row.

Bind off all sts in knit.

Rep along opposite edge.

On the 2 remaining Edges: With RS facing, pick up 164 sts evenly spaced along edge (68 sts for each square and 14 sts along already worked Edging on each side).

Work in Double Moss st for 2½" (6.5 cm), end with a RS row.

Bind off all sts in knit.

SUMMER & WINTER
Puffy Blanket in Two Versions

I have to admit this is my favorite design in this book. I set out with a mission: I wanted to create a blanket that would double as an ultra-thick, soft pad for baby to rest or play on. I tried many three-dimensional pattern stitches before settling on this broad field of puffy leaf-like motifs. The seed stitch edges are knit at the same time, so the richly-textured blanket is made all in one piece. It is shown here in two very different yarns, for different seasons. You could also make this blanket/mat by doubling a lighter weight yarn. No matter what size it turns out to be, it will become Mom's favorite. In 100% cotton, it would also make the most longwearing and absorbent bath wrap—or beach towel!—for the little one.

FINISHED MEASUREMENTS

Summer: Approximately 25" wide x 24½" high (63.5 cm x 62 cm)

Winter: Approximately 28" wide x 25" high (71 cm x 63.5 cm)

MATERIALS

**Summer Version -
SPUD AND CHLOË™
"Outer"**

(65% Wool, 35% Organic Cotton; 100 grams/60 yards)

   Color #7213 (Bubble): 7 hanks

**Winter Version -
BEROCCO®
"Peruvia® Quick"** SUPER BULKY 6

(100% Peruvian Highland Wool; 100 grams/103 yards)

   Color #9179 (Camote): 5 hanks

Straight knitting needles,

   size 13 (9 mm) **or** size needed
   to obtain gauge

Stitch markers

GAUGE

Over Seed st using "Outer" and size 13 needles:
10 sts and 14 rows = 4" (10 cm)
Over Seed st using "Peruvia Quick" and size 13 needles:
11 sts and 18 rows = 4" (10 cm)
Take time to save time, check your gauge.

Techniques used:
• K2 tog (*Fig. 8, page 119*)
• SSK (*Figs. 10a-c, page 120*)
• Slip 1 as if to **knit**, K2 tog, PSSO (*Figs. 12a & b, page 121*)

PATTERN STITCHES

SEED STITCH (Seed st): Odd number of sts
Row 1: K1, * P1, K1; rep from * across.
Rep Row 1 for Seed st.

PUFFY PATTERN: Multiple of 6 sts plus 5
Note: Stitch count does not remain the same. It can be checked on Rows 12 and 24.

Row 1 (RS): P5, * (K1, P1, K1, P1, K1) in next st to make 5 sts, P5; rep from * across.
Row 2: K5, * P5, K5; rep from * across.
Rows 3-8: Work the sts as they present themselves: Knit the knit sts and purl the purl sts.
Row 9: P5, * SSK, K1, K2 tog, P5; rep from * across.
Row 10: Work the sts as they present themselves: Knit the knit sts and purl the purl sts.
Row 11: P5, * slip 1, K2 tog, PSSO, P5; rep from * across.
Row 12: Knit across.
Row 13: P2, (K1, P1, K1, P1, K1) in next st to make 5 sts, * P5, (K1, P1, K1, P1, K1) in next st to make 5 sts; rep from * across, end P2.
Row 14: K2, P5, * K5, P5; rep from * across, end K2.
Rows 15-20: Work the sts as they present themselves: Knit the knit sts and purl the purl sts.
Row 21: P2, SSK, K1, K2 tog, * P5, SSK, K1, K2 tog; rep from * across, end P2.
Row 22: Work the sts as they present themselves: Knit the knit sts and purl the purl sts.
Row 23: P2, slip 1, K2 tog, PSSO, * P5, slip 1, K2 tog, PSSO; rep from * across, end P2.
Row 24 (WS): Knit across.
Rep Rows 1-24 for Puffy pattern.

BLANKET

Note: Instructions are written for Summer Version made using "Outer" with instructions for Winter Version made using "Peruvia Quick" in braces { }.

With straight needles, cast on 63{77} sts.

Beginning Border: Work in Seed st for 4" (10 cm).

Center Section (RS): Work 11{15} sts in Seed st as established, place marker (PM) *(see Markers, page 114)*, knit center 41{47} sts, PM, end work 11{15} sts in Seed st as established.

Next Row (WS): Work 11{15} sts in Seed st as established, slip marker, knit center 41{47} sts, slip marker, end work 11{15} sts in Seed st as established.

Next Row (RS): Work 11{15} sts in Seed st as established, slip marker, work Row 1 of Puffy pattern over center 41{47} sts, slip marker, end work 11{15} sts in Seed st as established.

Continue in patterns as established until center Puffy section is approximately square, ending with Row 12 or Row 24 of Puffy pattern, a WS row — 63{77} sts.

Next Row (RS): Work 11{15} sts in Seed st as established, remove marker, knit center 41{47} sts, remove marker, end work 11{15} sts in Seed st as established.

Ending Border: Work in Seed st over all 63{77} sts for 4" (10 cm), same number of rows as Beginning Border.

Bind off all sts in Seed st.

FINISHING
Weave in all ends and steam lightly.

TULIPS & BOWS
Pullover, Socks, and Blanket

For this very special updated layette set, bubbly texture and smooth lace tulips create a wonderful contrast. Ribbons add sheen and detail. For a modern look, I chose a very up-to-date pale citron green yarn. The slightly oversized pullover has a boxy full shape (even in the sleeves) that can be worn for a couple of years rather than just for a season! My favorite baby sock with diagonal ribs completes the look. Of course you could omit the ribbons that weave in and out of eyelets in the borders. Or you could replace them with little knitted cords. Cast on and bind off—that's how easy it is to make a narrow cord.

SIZES

To fit sizes 6{12-18-24} months
Sample worked in size 12 months.

FINISHED MEASUREMENTS

Pullover:
    Chest at underarm:
        22{26-28-30}"/56{66-71-76} cm
    Length: 11{12-13-14}"/
        28{30.5-33-35.5} cm
    Sleeve width at upper arm:
        11{12-13-14}"/
        28{30.5-33-35.5} cm
Blanket: 24" wide x 33" high
    (61 cm x 84 cm)

Size Note: Instructions for Pullover are written for size 6 months with sizes 12, 18 and 24 months in braces { }. Instructions will be easier to read if you circle all the numbers pertaining to your baby's size. If only one number is given, it applies to all sizes.

MATERIALS

ROWAN
"Belle Organic DK" **LIGHT 3**
(50% Organic Cotton/
50% Organic Wool;
50 grams/131 yards) in colors:
    Pullover and Socks:
    MC #016 (Cilantro):
        5{6-6-7} balls
    CC #013 (Moonflower): 1 ball
    ¼" (7 mm) wide Ribbon (Ivory)
        - 2 yards (1.83 meters)
    Blanket:
    MC #016 (Cilantro): 7 balls
    CC #013 (Moonflower): 1 ball
    ¼" (7 mm) wide Ribbon (Ivory)
        - 4 yards (3.66 meters)
Straight knitting needles, size 6 **or**
    size needed to obtain gauge
Double-pointed knitting needles
    (set of 5), size 6 (for Socks)
Stitch markers
Tapestry needle

GAUGE

Over Puffy Rib pattern
with size 6 needles:
24 sts and 30 rows = 4" (10 cm)
Take time to save time, check your gauge.

Techniques used:
• YO *(Figs. 5a-d, page 117)*
• K2 tog *(Fig. 8, page 119)*
• P2 tog *(Fig. 9, page 119)*
• SSK *(Figs. 10a-c, page 120)*
• P3 tog *(Fig. 11, page 121)*
• Slip 2 tog as if to **knit**, K1, P2SSO *(Figs. 13a & b, page 122)*

PATTERN STITCHES

STOCKINETTE STITCH (St st):
Any number of sts
Knit RS rows, Purl WS rows.

P3/K3 RIB PATTERN: Multiple of 6 sts plus 3
Row 1 (RS): P3, * K3, P3; rep from * across.
Row 2: K3, * P3, K3; rep from * across.
Rep Rows 1 and 2 for P3/K3 rib pattern.

PUFFY RIB PATTERN: Multiple of 6 sts plus 3
Rows 1 and 3 (RS): P1, K1, P1, * K3, P1, K1, P1; rep from * across.
Rows 2 and 6: Work sts as they appear: Knit the knit sts and purl the purl sts.
Row 4: K1, P1, K1, * YO, P3 tog, YO, K1, P1, K1; rep from * across.
Rows 5 and 7: K3, * P1, K1, P1, K3; rep from * across.
Row 8: YO, P3 tog, YO, * K1, P1, K1, YO, P3 tog, YO; rep from * across.
Rep Rows 1-8 for Puffy Rib pattern.

TULIP BORDER: Multiple of 20 sts plus 1
Row 1 (WS) and all other WS rows: Purl across.
Row 2: K5, * K2 tog, YO, K1, YO, K2 tog, K1, SSK, YO, K1, YO, SSK, K9; rep from * across, end last rep K5.
Row 4: K4, * K2 tog, YO, K2, YO, K2 tog, K1, SSK, YO, K2, YO, SSK, K7; rep from * across, end last rep K4.

Row 6: K3, * K2 tog, YO, K3, YO, K2 tog, K1, SSK, YO, K3, YO, SSK, K5; rep from * across, end last rep K3.

Row 8: K2, * K2 tog, YO, K4, YO, K2 tog, K1, SSK, YO, K4, YO, SSK, K3; rep from * across, end last rep K2.

Row 10: K1, * K2 tog, YO, K5, YO, K2 tog, K1, SSK, YO, K5, YO, SSK, K1; rep from * across.

Row 12: K2, * YO, K2 tog, K2, (K2 tog, YO) twice, K1, (YO, SSK) twice, K2, SSK, YO, K3; rep from * across, end last rep K2.

Row 14: K2, * YO, K2 tog, K1, (K2 tog, YO) twice, K3, (YO, SSK) twice, K1, SSK, YO, K3; rep from * across, end last rep K2.

Row 16: K2, * YO, K2 tog twice, YO, K2 tog, YO, K5, YO, SSK, YO, SSK twice, YO, K3; rep from * across, end last rep K2.

Row 18: K2, * YO, slip 2, K1, P2SSO, YO, K2 tog, YO, K7, YO, SSK, YO, slip 2, K1, P2SSO, YO, K3; rep from * across, end last rep K2.

Row 20: K2, * K2 tog, YO, K2, YO, K2 tog, K5, SSK, YO, K2, YO, SSK, K3; rep from * across, end last rep K2.

Row 22: K6, * YO, K2 tog, K5, SSK, YO, K 11; rep from * across, end last rep K6.

Row 24: K6, * YO, K2 tog twice, YO, K1, YO, SSK twice, YO, K 11; rep from * across, end last rep K6.

Row 26: K6, * YO, slip 2, K1, P2SSO, YO, K3, YO, slip 2, K1, P2SSO, YO, K 11; rep from * across, end last rep K6.

Row 28: Knit across.

PULLOVER
BACK

With straight needles and MC, cast on 67{79-85-91} sts.

Next Row (RS): K2 (St st edge sts), work in P3/K3 Rib pattern over center 63{75-81-87} sts, end K2 (St st edge sts).

Work even as established until piece measures 2" (5 cm), end with a WS row.

Next Row (RS): K2 (St st edge sts), work in Puffy Rib pattern over center 63{75-81-87} sts, end K2 (St st edge sts).

Work even as established until piece measures 10½{11½-12½-13½}"/ 26.5{29-32-34.5} cm, end with Row 2 or Row 6.

Back Neck Shaping: Mark center 31{31-35-37} sts.

Work to center 31{31-35-37} sts, join a second ball of yarn and bind off center sts, work as established to end — 18{24-25-27} sts remain each side.

Keeping one st at each Neck edge in St st, working both sides at the same time with separate balls of yarn, work even for 3 rows more.

Bind off remaining 18{24-25-27} sts each side for shoulders.

FRONT

Work same as for Back until piece measures 8{9-10-11}"/ 20.5{23-25.5-28} cm, end with a WS row.

Front Neck Shaping: Mark center 31{31-35-37} sts.
Work to center 31{31-35-37} sts, join a second ball of yarn and bind off center sts, work as established to end — 18{24-25-27} sts remain each side.

Keeping one st at each Neck edge in St st, working both sides at the same time with separate balls of yarn, work even until neckline measures 3" (7.5 cm), end with Row 2 or Row 6.

Bind off remaining 18{24-25-27} sts each side for shoulders.

SLEEVE (Make 2)

With straight needles and MC, cast on 67{73-79-85} sts.

Next Row (RS): K2 (St st edge sts), work in P3/K3 Rib pattern over center 63{69-75-81} sts, end K2 (St st edge sts).

Work even as established until piece measures 2" (5 cm), end with a WS row.

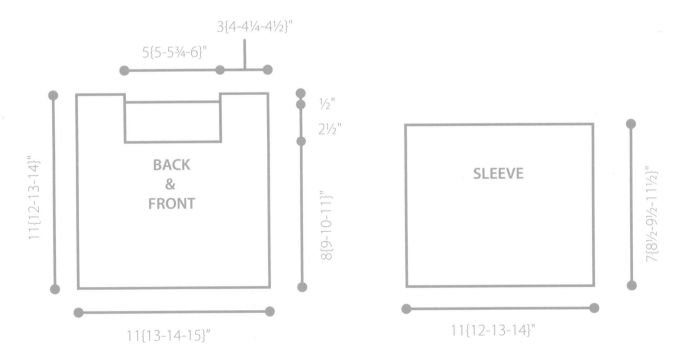

3{4-4¼-4½}"

5{5-5¾-6}"

11{12-13-14}"

½"

2½"

8{9-10-11}"

BACK & FRONT

SLEEVE

7{8½-9½-11½}"

11{13-14-15}"

11{12-13-14}"

Next Row (RS): K2 (St st edge sts), work in Puffy Rib pattern over center 63{69-75-81} sts, end K2 (St st edge sts).

Work even as established until piece measures 7{8$\frac{1}{2}$-9$\frac{1}{2}$-11$\frac{1}{2}$}"/ 18{21.5-24-29} cm, end with Row 2 or Row 6.

Bind off all sts in pattern.

FINISHING

Sew right shoulder seam.

Neckline Trim: With RS facing, using straight needles and CC, pick up 16 sts evenly spaced from left shoulder to Front Neck *(Figs. 14a & b, page 123)*, 2 sts in corner (mark these sts), 30{30-34-38} sts evenly spaced across Front Neck edge, 2 sts in corner (mark these sts), 16 sts evenly spaced across to right shoulder, then 32{32-36-40} sts evenly spaced across Back Neck edge — 98{98-106-114} sts.

Knit WS row.

Next (eyelet) Row (RS): (K2, K2 tog, YO) 4 times to marked sts, K2 corner sts, YO, K2 tog, (K2, K2 tog, YO) 7{7-8-9} times to marked sts, K2 corner sts, YO, K2 tog, K2, (K2 tog, YO, K2) 11{11-12-13} times to end.

Purl WS row.

Next (decrease) Row (RS): P 15, K2 tog, SSK, P 28{28-32-36}, K2 tog, SSK, purl to end — 94{94-102-110} sts.

Change to MC and purl WS row.

Next (decrease) Row (RS): P 14, K2 tog, SSK, P 26{26-30-34}, K2 tog, SSK, purl to end — 90{90-98-106} sts.

Bind off all sts in knit on WS.

Sew left shoulder seam.

Cut a length of ribbon 32-34" (81.5-86.5 cm) long. Beginning at front left corner, thread through eyelets and tie in a bow at corner.

Mark 5$\frac{1}{2}${6-6$\frac{1}{2}$-7} "/ 14{15-16.5-18} cm down from shoulder on Front and Back.

Sew Sleeves between markers. Sew Sleeve and side seams.

BLANKET

With straight needles and MC, cast on 123 sts.

* Work in Puffy Rib pattern for 20 rows, ending with Row 4 of pattern.

Knit RS row, decreasing 20 sts evenly spaced across *(see Increasing or Decreasing Evenly Across a Row, page 118)* — 103 sts.

Next Row (WS): Keeping first and last st in St st, work Row 1 of Tulip Border over center 101 sts.

Work even in pattern until Row 28 of Border is complete, ending with a RS row.

Purl WS row, increasing 20 sts evenly spaced across — 123 sts.

Rep from * 3 times more (total of 4 Tulip Lace Borders), then work in Puffy Rib pattern for 20 rows, ending with Row 4 of pattern.

Bind off all sts in pattern.

FINISHING

Note: Work trim on short edges first.

Short Edge Trim: With RS of cast on edge facing, using straight needles and CC, pick up 104 sts evenly spaced along edge.

Row 1 (WS): Knit across.

Row 2 (eyelet): K4, * YO, K2 tog, K3; rep from * across.

Rows 3 and 4: Purl across.

Row 5: Change to MC and purl across.

Rows 6-8: Knit across.

Rows 9-11: Purl across.

Rows 12-14: Knit across.

Rows 15-17: Purl across.

Rows 18 and 19: Knit across.

Bind off all sts in knit on RS row.

Repeat Short Edge Trim along bound off edge.

Long Edge Trim: With RS facing, using straight needles and CC, pick up 169 sts evenly spaced along long edge.

Work trim as for Short Edge.

Repeat Long Edge Trim along opposite long edge.

Thread large tapestry needle with ribbon.
Beginning on WS, weave a length of ribbon along short edge through eyelets, ending on WS.
Cut ribbon and pin at back; sew in place with sewing needle and thread.

Rep on remaining 3 sides.

Cut 4 pieces of ribbon approximately 8" (20.5 cm) long and tie into a bow.
Sew bows at center of each edge on woven ribbon.

SOCKS
To fit sizes 6{12-18-24} months

PATTERN STITCH: Multiple of 4 sts
Rnds 1-4: * K2, P2; rep from * around.
Rnds 5-8: * K1, P2, K1; rep from * around.
Rnds 9-12: * P2, K2; rep from * around.
Rnds 13-16: * P1, K2, P1; rep from * around.
Rep Rnds 1-16 for pattern.

LEG
With dpns and MC, cast on 36 sts and divide sts evenly onto 4 dpns (9 sts on each needle) *(Fig. 2, page 115)*.

Work Rnds 1-4 of Pattern st.

Next (eyelet) Rnd: * K2, YO, P2 tog; rep from * around.

Continue with Rnd 5 of Pattern st and work through Rnd 16, then rep Rnds 1-16 until piece measures 6" (15 cm).

TOE
Rnd 1: Change to CC and knit around.

Rnd 2: * K1, SSK, K6; rep from * around — 32 sts.

Rnd 3: Knit around.

Rnd 4: * K2, SSK, K4; rep from * around — 28 sts.

Rnd 5: Knit around.

Rnd 6: * K3, SSK, K2; rep from * around — 24 sts.

Rnd 7: * K4, SSK; rep from * around — 20 sts.

Divide sts evenly on 2 needles and graft together *(Figs. 17a & b, page 125)*.

Cut a length of ribbon 18" (45.5 cm) long. Thread ribbon through eyelets and tie in a bow.

VALENTINE
A Textured Heart-Patterned Cardigan

Sometimes I like to transform an adult garment idea to "pint-size," as I did with the notion of a traditional Chinese jacket with overlapping fronts, reduced for baby! Once again, I wanted to do a heart motif, so I hunted for valentine-patterned colorwork. For vertical stripes, the body piece was knitted side-to-side. The stranded two-color "heart" patterned borders were picked up and worked downward. I chose a warm, high quality wool/mohair blend—one that is sure to stand the test of time and many careful hand washings. The bright colors of this sweater speak of Baby's high energy, as would the stark contrast of black and white! For softer effects, imagine this piece in pastels or in shades of grey and brown for earthy warmth.

SIZES
To fit sizes 6{12-18-24} months
Sample worked in size 12 months.

FINISHED MEASUREMENTS
Chest at underarm:
  25{28-31-33}"/
  63.5{71-78.5-84} cm
Length: 11¹/₂{12-12¹/₂-13}"/
  29{30.5-32-33} cm
Sleeve width at upper arm:
  11{12-13-14}"/
  28{30.5-33-35.5} cm

Size Note: Instructions are written for size 6 months with sizes 12, 18 and 24 months in braces { }. Instructions will be easier to read if you circle all the numbers pertaining to your baby's size. If only one number is given, it applies to all sizes.

MATERIALS
NASHUA HANDKNITS
"Julia"
(50% Wool, 25% Mohair, 25% Alpaca; 50 grams/93 yards) in colors:
  A #NHJ1054 (Sunflower):
    3{3-3-4} skeins
  B #NHJ5084 (Zinnia Pink):
    1{2-2-2} skein(s)
  C #NHJ3961 (Ladies Mantle):
    1{1-1-2} skein(s)
  D #NHJ5178 (Lupine): 1 skein
  E #NHJ1784 (Gourd): 1 skein
  F #NHJ2083 (Magenta): 1 skein
Straight knitting needles, sizes 7
  (4.5 mm) **and** 8 (5 mm) **or** sizes
  needed to obtain gauge
Yarn needle
1³/₄" (44 mm) Toggle button - 1

GAUGE
Over Striped pattern
with size 7 needles:
19 sts and 24 rows = 4" (10 cm)
Over Charted pattern
with size 8 needles:
20 sts and 22 rows = 4" (10 cm)
Take time to save time, check your gauge.

Technique used:
• Changing Colors *(Figs. 4a & b, page 116)*
• Increases *(page 118)*

PATTERN STITCHES
SEED STITCH: Even number of sts
Row 1: * K1, P1; rep from* across.
Row 2: * P1, K1; rep from* across.
Rep Rows 1 and 2 for Seed st.

STRIPED PATTERN: Multiple of 2 sts
Row 1 (RS): With A, knit across.
Rows 2-4: Work in Seed st.
Row 5 (RS): * K1 A, K1 B; rep from * across.
Row 6: With B, purl across.
Row 7: With B, knit across.
Row 8 (WS): With C, purl across.
Rows 9 and 10: Work in Seed st.
Row 11 (RS): * K1 C, K1 D; rep from * across.
Row 12: With D, purl across.
Row 13: With D, knit across.
Row 14 (WS): With A, purl across.
Rows 15-17: Work in Seed st.
Row 18 (WS): * P1 A, P1 E; rep from * across.
Row 19: With E, knit across.
Row 20: With E, purl across.
Row 21 (RS): With C, knit across.
Rows 22 and 23: Work in Seed st.
Row 24 (WS): * P1 C, P1 F; rep from * across.
Row 25: With F, knit across.
Row 26: With F, purl across.
Rep Rows 1-26 for Striped pattern.

CARDIGAN
BODY

Note: Body is worked side-to-side, and then the stranded color work border pattern chart is picked up along lower unshaped edge and knitted down.

With size 7 needles and A, cast on 12 sts.

Work in Striped pattern for 2 rows, end with a WS row.

Shape Right Front Edge: Keeping in pattern cast on 2 sts at the beginning of the next 13{14-15-16} RS rows using backward loop cast on *(Fig. 1, page 114)* — 38{40-42-44} sts.

Work even in pattern until piece measures 2^1/$_2${3-3^1/$_2$-4}"/ 6.5{7.5-9-10} cm from last cast on, end with a WS row.

Shape Right Armhole (RS): Bind off 26{28-30-32} sts, work to end — 12 sts remain.

Next Row (WS): Work 12 sts, then cast on 26{28-30-32} sts — 38{40-42-44} sts.

Work even in pattern until piece measures 2^1/$_2${3-3^1/$_2$-4}"/ 6.5{7.5-9-10} cm from armhole cast on, end with a WS row.

Shape Back Neck (RS): Bind off 2 sts, work as established to end — 36{38-40-42} sts.

Work even in pattern until piece measures 6" (15 cm) from neckline bind off, end with a WS row.

Next Row (RS): Cast on 2 sts, work as established to end — 38{40-42-44} sts.

Work even in pattern until piece measures 2^1/$_2${3-3^1/$_2$-4}"/ 6.5{7.5-9-10} cm from neckline cast on, end with a WS row.

Shape Left Armhole (RS): Bind off 26{28-30-32} sts, work to end — 12 sts remain.

Next Row (WS): Work 12 sts, then cast on 26{28-30-32} sts — 38{40-42-44} sts.

Work even in pattern until piece measures 2^1/$_2${3-3^1/$_2$-4}"/ 6.5{7.5-9-10} cm from armhole cast on, end with a WS row.

Shape Left Front Edge (RS): Keeping in pattern, bind off 2 sts at the beginning of the next 13{14-15-16} RS rows — 12 sts.

Work even for 2 rows.

Bind off all sts in pattern.

Lower Border: With RS facing, using size 8 needles and C, pick up 126{142-156-166} sts evenly spaced along the lower edge of body piece *(Figs. 14a & b, page 123)*.

Next Row (WS): Following Border pattern chart, begin where indicated, marking chart where last st was worked and begin all RS rows at this st.

Work Border pattern chart until all 22 rows are complete.

With E bind off all sts in purl.

Trim: With RS of Border facing, using size 7 needles and A, pick up 127{137-147-157} sts evenly spaced across bind off row.

Knit 1 row, purl 1 row, knit 1 row.

Change to F and bind off all sts in knit.

SLEEVE (Make 2)
Note: Sleeve is worked side-to-side, and then the stranded color work border pattern chart is picked up along one side and knitted down.

With size 7 needles and A, cast on 22 sts.

Work in Striped pattern until piece measures 11{12-13-14}"/ 28{30.5-33-35.5} cm.

Bind off all sts in pattern.

Lower Border: With RS facing, using size 8 needles and C, pick up 40{43-46-49} sts evenly spaced along the long side of sleeve edge.

Next Row (WS): Following Border pattern chart, begin where indicated, marking chart where last st was worked and begin all RS rows at this st.

Work Border pattern chart until all 22 rows are complete.

With E bind off all sts in purl.

Trim: With RS of Border facing, using size 7 needles and A, pick up 36{39-42-45} sts evenly spaced across bind off row.

Knit 1 row, purl 1 row, knit 1 row.

Change to F and bind off all sts in knit.

BORDER PATTERN

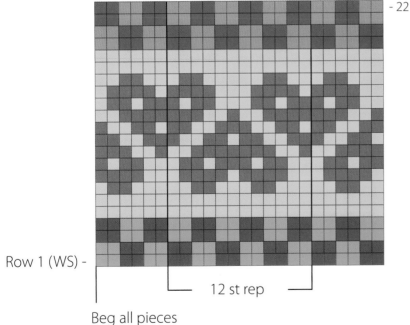

- 22

Row 1 (WS) -

12 st rep

Beg all pieces

COLOR KEY
Chart is worked in St st.
Work chart from left to right on WS rows and right to left on RS rows.

■ A
■ B
■ C
■ D
■ E
■ F

FINISHING

Steam pieces lightly.
Sew Fronts to Back at shoulders.

Sew Sleeve seams.
Sew Sleeves into armholes.

Edging: With size 7 needles and A, pick up 68{70-72-74} sts evenly spaced along Right Front edge, 25{29-33-37} sts evenly spaced across Back neck and 68{70-72-74} sts evenly spaced along Left Front edge — 161{169-177-185} sts.

Knit WS row.

Purl RS row increasing one st at oint of neck shaping.

Knit WS row.

Change to F and bind off all sts in knit.

Button Loop: With size 7 needles and E, cast on 10 sts.

Bind off all sts in knit on next row.

Sew as a loop at lower V-Neckline of Right Front.

Sew button to Left Front opposite loop.

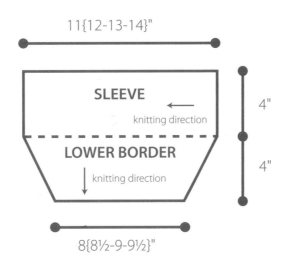

11{12-13-14}"

SLEEVE

knitting direction

4"

LOWER BORDER

4"

knitting direction

8{8½-9-9½}"

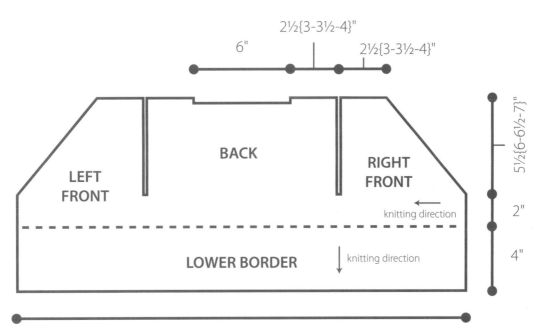

2½{3-3½-4}"

6"

2½{3-3½-4}"

LEFT
FRONT

BACK

RIGHT
FRONT

5½{6-6½-7}"

knitting direction

2"

LOWER BORDER

knitting direction

4"

25{28-31-33}"

GENERAL INSTRUCTIONS

ABBREVIATIONS

BC	Back Cross
CC	Contrasting Color
cm	centimeters
cn	cable needle
dpn(s)	double-pointed needle(s)
FC	Front Cross
K	knit
LH	Left Hand
LT	Left Twist
M1	Make One
MC	Main Color
mm	millimeters
P	purl
PM	place marker
PSSO	pass slipped stitch over
P2SSO	pass 2 slipped stitches over
rep(s)	repeat(s)
Rev	Reverse
RH	Right Hand
Rnd(s)	Round(s)
RS	Right Side
RT	Right Twist
SSK	slip, slip, knit
St st	Stockinette stitch
st(s)	stitch(es)
tbl	through back loop(s)
tog	together
WS	Wrong Side
YO	yarn over(s)

SYMBOLS & TERMS

* — work instructions following * as many **more** times as indicated in addition to the first time.

( ) or [ ] — work enclosed instructions **as many** times as specified by the number immediately following **or** work all enclosed instructions in the stitch indicated **or** contains explanatory remarks.

long dash — the number(s) given after a long dash (—) at the end of a row or round denote(s) the number of stitches you should have on that row or round.

work even — work without increasing or decreasing in the established pattern.

GAUGE

Exact gauge is **essential** for proper fit. Before beginning your project, make a sample swatch in the yarn and needles specified. After completing the swatch, measure it, counting your stitches and rows carefully. If your swatch is larger or smaller than specified, **make another, changing needle size to get the correct gauge**. Keep trying until you find the size needles that will give you the specified gauge. Once proper gauge is obtained, measure width of piece approximately every 3" (7.5 cm) to be sure gauge remains consistent.

If you have more rows per inch than specified, use a larger size needle for the purl rows; if fewer, use a smaller size needle for the purl rows.

KNIT TERMINOLOGY	
UNITED STATES	**INTERNATIONAL**
gauge =	tension
bind off =	cast off
yarn over (YO) =	yarn forward (yfwd) **or**
	yarn around needle (yrn)

Yarn Weight Symbol & Names	LACE **0**	SUPER FINE **1**	FINE **2**	LIGHT **3**	MEDIUM **4**	BULKY **5**	SUPER BULKY **6**
Type of Yarns in Category	Fingering, size 10 crochet thread	Sock, Fingering, Baby	Sport, Baby	DK, Light Worsted	Worsted, Afghan, Aran	Chunky, Craft, Rug	Bulky, Roving
Knit Gauge Range* in Stockinette St to 4" (10 cm)	33-40** sts	27-32 sts	23-26 sts	21-24 sts	16-20 sts	12-15 sts	6-11 sts
Advised Needle Size Range	000-1	1 to 3	3 to 5	5 to 7	7 to 9	9 to 11	11 and larger

*GUIDELINES ONLY: The chart above reflects the most commonly used gauges and needle sizes for specific yarn categories.

** Lace weight yarns are usually knitted on larger needles to create lacy openwork patterns. Accordingly, a gauge range is difficult to determine. Always follow the gauge stated in your pattern.

KNITTING NEEDLES																		
U.S.	0	1	2	3	4	5	6	7	8	9	10	10½	11	13	15	17	19	35	50
U.K.	13	12	11	10	9	8	7	6	5	4	3	2	1	00	000	---	---	---	---
Metric - mm	2	2.25	2.75	3.25	3.5	3.75	4	4.5	5	5.5	6	6.5	8	9	10	12.75	15	19	25

■□□□ **BEGINNER**	Projects for first-time knitters using basic knit and purl stitches. Minimal shaping.
■■□□ **EASY**	Projects using basic stitches, repetitive stitch patterns, simple color changes, and simple shaping and finishing.
■■■□ **INTERMEDIATE**	Projects with a variety of stitches, such as basic cables and lace, simple intarsia, double-pointed needles and knitting in the round needle techniques, mid-level shaping and finishing.
■■■■ **EXPERIENCED**	Projects using advanced techniques and stitches, such as short rows, fair isle, more intricate intarsia, cables, lace patterns, and numerous color changes.

HINTS

As in all garments, good finishing techniques make a big difference in the quality of the piece. Do not tie knots. Always start a new ball at the beginning of a row, leaving ends long enough to weave in later. With **wrong** side facing, weave the needle through several stitches, then reverse the direction and weave it back through several stitches. When the ends are secure, clip them off close to work.

MARKERS

As a convenience to you, we have used markers to help distinguish the beginning of a pattern or round or to mark placement of decreases or increases. Place a marker as instructed. You may use purchased markers or tie a length of contrasting color yarn around the needle. When you reach a marker on each row or round, slip it from the left needle to the right needle; remove it when no longer needed.

ZEROS

To consolidate the length of an involved pattern, Zeros are sometimes used so that all sizes can be combined. For example, knit 0{1-2} sts means the first size would do nothing, the second size would K1, and the largest size would K2.

BACKWARD LOOP CAST ON

Make a loop and place it on the needle *(Fig. 1)*.

Fig. 1

USING DOUBLE-POINTED NEEDLES

When working too few stitches to use a circular needle, double-pointed needles are required. Divide the stitches into fourths and slip one-fourth of the stitches onto each of 4 double-pointed needles, forming a square *(Fig. 2)*. With the fifth needle, knit across the stitches on the first needle. You will now have an empty needle with which to knit the stitches from the next needle. Work the first stitch of each needle firmly to prevent gaps.

Fig. 2

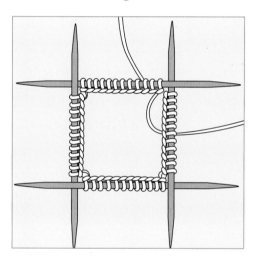

THROUGH BACK LOOP
(abbreviated tbl)

When instructed to knit or purl into the back loop of a stitch *(Fig. 3)*, the result will be twisted stitches.

Fig. 3

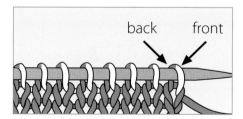

CHANGING COLORS

Wind small amounts of each color onto a bobbin to keep the different color yarns from tangling. You'll need one bobbin for each color change, except when there are so few stitches of the new color that it would be easier to carry the unused color **loosely** across the back *(Fig. 4a)*. Always keep the bobbins on the **wrong** side of the garment. When changing colors, always pick up the new color yarn from **beneath** the dropped yarn and keep the color which has just been worked to the left *(Fig. 4b)*. This will prevent holes in the finished piece. Take extra care to keep your tension even. For proper fit, it is essential to maintain gauge when following charts.

Fig. 4a

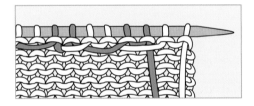

Fig. 4b

YARN OVERS

A yarn over *(abbreviated YO)* is simply placing the yarn over the right needle creating an extra stitch. Since the yarn over produces a hole in the knit fabric, it is used for a lacy effect. One the row following a yarn over, you must be careful to keep it on the needle and treat it as a stitch by knitting or purling it as instructed.

To make a yarn over, you'll loop the yarn over the needle like you would to knit or purl a stitch, bringing it either to the front or to the back of the piece so that it'll be ready to work the next stitch, creating a new stitch on the needle as follows:

After a knit stitch, before a knit stitch
Bring the yarn forward **between** the needles, then back **over** the top of the right-hand needle, so that it is now in position to knit the next stitch *(Fig. 5a)*.

After a purl stitch, before a purl stitch
Take the yarn **over** the right-hand needle to the back, then forward **under** it, so that it is now in position to purl the next stitch *(Fig. 5b)*.

After a knit stitch, before a purl stitch
Bring the yarn forward between the needles, then back **over** the top of the right-hand needle and forward **between** the needles again, so that it is now in position to purl the next stitch *(Fig. 5c)*.

After a purl stitch, before a knit stitch
Take the yarn **over** the right-hand needle to the back, so that it is now in position to knit the next stitch *(Fig. 5d)*.

Fig. 5a

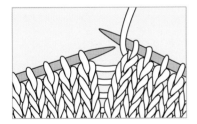

Fig. 5b

Fig. 5c

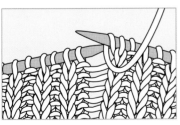

Fig. 5d

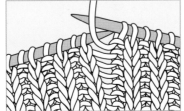

INCREASING OR DECREASING EVENLY ACROSS A ROW

Add one to the number of increases/decreases required and divide that number into the number of stitches on the needle. Subtract one from the result for increases or subtract two from the result for decreases, and the new number is the approximately number of stitches to be worked between each increase/decrease. Adjust the number as needed.

INCREASES

The type of increase used depends on the stitch needed to maintain the pattern.

BAR INCREASE

The bar increase uses one stitch to make two stitches. You will have two stitches on the right needle for the one stitch worked off the left needle.

KNIT: Knit the next stitch but do **not** slip the old stitch off the left needle. Insert the right needle into the **back** loop of the **same** stitch and knit it *(Fig. 6a)*, then slip the old stitch off the left needle.

PURL: Purl the next stitch but do **not** slip the old stitch off the left needle. Insert the right needle into the **back** loop of the **same** stitch and purl it *(Fig. 6b)*, then slip the old stitch off the left needle.

Fig. 6a

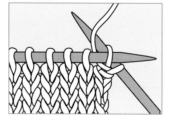

Fig. 6b

MAKE 1 (abbreviated M1)

Insert the left needle under the horizontal strand between the stitches from the **front** *(Fig. 7a)*, then knit into the **back** of the strand *(Fig. 7b)*.

Fig. 7a  Fig. 7b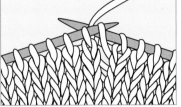

DECREASES

KNIT 2 TOGETHER *(abbreviated K2 tog)*

Insert the right needle into the **front** of the first two stitches on the left needle as if to **knit** *(Fig. 8)*, then **knit** them together as if they were one stitch.

Fig. 8

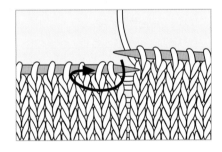

PURL 2 TOGETHER *(abbreviated P2 tog)*

Insert the right needle into the **front** of the first two stitches on the left needle as if to **purl** *(Fig. 9)*, then **purl** them together as if they were one stitch.

Fig. 9

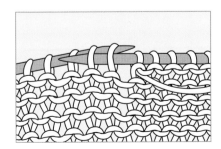

SLIP, SLIP, KNIT (abbreviated SSK)

Separately slip two stitches as if to **knit** *(Fig. 10a)*. Insert the **left** needle into the **front** of both slipped stitches *(Fig. 10b)* and then **knit** them together as if they were one stitch *(Fig. 10c)*.

Fig. 10a

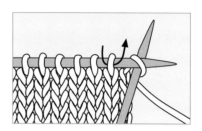

Fig. 10b

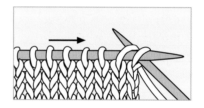

Fig. 10c

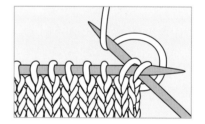

PURL 3 TOGETHER *(abbreviated P3 tog)*

Insert the right needle into the **front** of the first three stitches on the left needle as if to **purl** *(Fig. 11)*, then **purl** them together as if they were one stitch.

Fig. 11

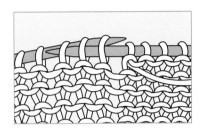

SLIP 1, KNIT 2 TOGETHER, PASS SLIPPED STITCH OVER
(abbreviated slip 1, K2 tog, PSSO)

Slip one stitch as if to **knit** *(Fig. 12a)*, then knit the next two stitches together *(Fig. 8, page 119)*. With the left needle, bring the slipped stitch over the stitch just made *(Fig. 12b)* and off the needle.

Fig. 12a

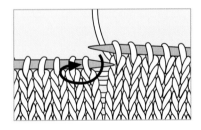

Fig. 12b

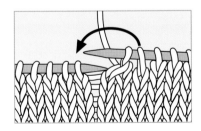

SLIP 2, KNIT 1, PASS 2 SLIPPED STITCHES OVER *(abbreviated slip 2, K1, P2SSO)*

Slip two stitches together as if to **knit** *(Fig. 13a)*, then knit the next stitch. With the left needle, bring both slipped stitches over the knit stitch *(Fig. 13b)* and off the needle.

Fig. 13a

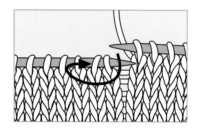

Fig. 13b

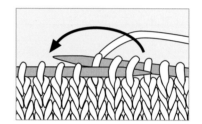

PICKING UP STITCHES

When instructed to pick up stitches, insert the needle from the **front** to the **back** under two strands at the edge of the worked piece. Put the yarn around the needle as if to **knit**, then bring the needle with the yarn back through the stitch to the right side, resulting in a stitch on the needle *(Figs. 14a & b)*. Repeat this along the edge, picking up the required number of stitches.

A crochet hook may be helpful to pull yarn through.

Fig. 14a

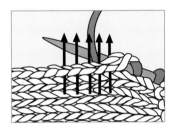

Fig. 14b

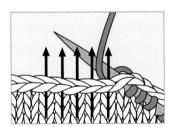

3-NEEDLE BIND OFF

Holding pieces with **right** sides together and needles parallel to each other, insert a third needle as if to **knit** into the first stitch on the front needle **and** into the first stitch on the back needle *(Fig. 15)*. Knit these two stitches together and slip them off the needles, * knit the next stitch on each needle together and slip them off the needles. To bind off, insert one left needle into the first stitch on the right needle and pull the first stitch over the second stitch and off the right needle; repeat from * across until all of the stitches have been bound off.

Fig. 15

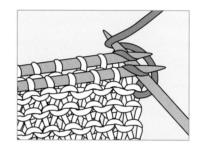

SEWING SEAMS

With the **right** side of both pieces facing you and edges even, sew through both sides once to secure the seam. Insert the needle under the bar **between** the first and second stitches on the row and pull the yarn through *(Fig. 16)*. Insert the needle under the next bar on the second side. Repeat from side-to-side, being careful to match rows. If the edges are different lengths, it may be necessary to insert the needle under two bars at one edge.

Fig. 16

GRAFTING

Thread the yarn needle with the long end. Hold the threaded yarn needle on the right-hand side of the work.

Work in the following sequence, pulling the yarn through as if to knit or as if to purl with even tension and keeping the yarn under the points of the needles to avoid tangling and extra loops.

Step 1: **Purl** first stitch on **front** needle, leave on *(Fig. 17a)*.

Step 2: **Knit** first stitch on **back** needle, leave on *(Fig. 17b)*.

Step 3: **Knit** first stitch on **front** needle, slip off.

Step 4: **Purl** next stitch on **front** needle, leave on.

Step 5: **Purl** first stitch on **back** needle, slip off.

Step 6: **Knit** next stitch on **back** needle, leave on.

Repeat Steps 3-6 across until one stitch remains on each needle, then repeat Steps 3 and 5.

Fig. 17a

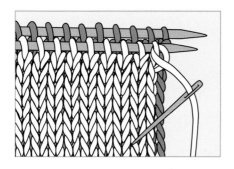

Fig. 17b

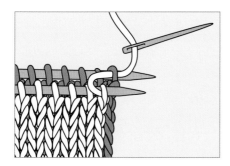

POM-POM

Cut a piece of cardboard 3" (7.5 cm) and as long as you want the diameter of your finished pom-pom to be. Wind the yarn around the cardboard until it is approximately ½" (12 mm) thick in the middle *(Fig. 18a)*. Carefully slip the yarn off the cardboard and firmly tie an 18" (45.5 cm) length of yarn around the middle *(Fig. 18b)*. Leave yarn ends long enough to attach the pom-pom. Cut the loops on both ends and trim the pom-pom into a smooth ball *(Fig. 18c)*.

Fig. 18a

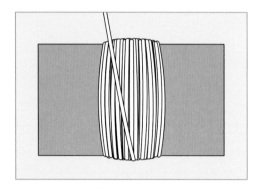

Fig. 18b

Fig. 18c

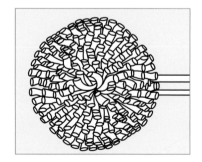

BASIC CROCHET STITCHES
CHAIN

To work a chain stitch, begin with a slip knot on the hook. Bring the yarn **over** the hook from back to front, catching the yarn with the hook and turning the hook slightly toward you to keep the yarn from slipping off. Draw the yarn through the slip knot *(Fig. 19)* (**first chain stitch made**).

Fig. 19

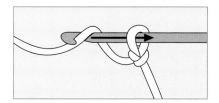

SLIP STITCH

To work a slip stitch, insert the hook in the stitch indicated, YO and draw through stitch and through loop on hook *(Fig. 20)* (**slip stitch made**).

Fig. 20

CARING FOR BABY'S HEIRLOOM KNITS

I have never understood the common assertion that all baby sweaters should be made of machine-washable yarns. Why shouldn't babies enjoy the same fibers adults do? Baby sweaters are far easier to wash than larger sweaters!

A baby or toddler sweater is small and therefore easy to care for, even if made in precious fibers. Here's how I do it. (Forewarning—don't let a sweater get extra dirty before you wash it. Take the time to address dirt before it gets embedded with time.)

Fill a small sink with cool water and add a little mild liquid soap-- you can use Woolite, but I most often use a little mild shampoo. Dunk the sweater to be sure it is fully wet, taking care not to twist or, heaven forbid, wring the fabric. Let it soak for about 5 minutes, then let the water drain from the sink.

Squeeze the sweater very gently to remove excess water. Then roll it in a small towel and squeeze the water out. Carefully pat the little sweater into shape on a thick dry towel. Do not flatten the texture of the fabric—with your fingers, pat the sweater to a smaller shape than it might have when dry. Do not stretch it to a larger size! Let it dry completely before removing from the towel.

Sometimes sweaters are fuller and softer after the first wash. Little sweaters dry fast, and soon baby will be wearing her treasure again!

— Deborah Newton